"When we're stressed out or feel as though there are too many things to do in our lives, many of us stop paying attention to the things that might make us feel and function better. This play-book provides the tools to form daily habits that help us thrive even during times of stress, allowing us to better connect with ourselves and others in our life."

**–Kimberly Williams, President & CEO at Vibrant Emotional Health**

"Working in recovery, I know how important daily reminders can be in one's journey to healing and sobriety. The Self!sh Playbook provides a personal tool to re-calibrate what is important and encourages mental fitness which is often overlooked in today's fast-paced world."

**—Gary Mendell, founder & CEO, Shatterproof**

"As a retired Olympic athlete and someone who now works in the field of mental performance, I love the idea of a playbook that keeps our guiding principles top of mind."

**– Nicole Davis, Psy.D., 2x Olympic Medalist, TEDx Speaker and Mindset Coach at Finding Mastery**

"Self!sh is a practical, easy accessible, step-by-step workbook that addresses where we are, where we want to be, and how to get there. Enjoy the experience of learning more about yourself and becoming the person that you deserve to be."

**–Antonio E. Puente, PhD 125th President, American Psychological Association and Board of Directors, Give an Hour**

"A great way to love on yourself so that you can let your love shine out into the world."

**–Miles Borrero, Author of *Beautiful Monster*, Yoga Teacher**

"I wholehearted recommend this read to anyone yearning for personal growth, fulfillment, and a deeper understanding of one-self. *Self!sh* is an invaluable guide on the journey to self-discovery and a testament to the transformative power that lies within each of us."

**–AJ Vaden, CEO and Co-Founder Brand Builders Group**

"*Self!sh* is an excellent contribution to the field of wellness. Paying attention to our mental health is good for us—actively working on our well being every day...even better!"

**–Barbara Van Dahlen, PhD, Founder & Former CEO, Give an Hour; Co-Founder & CEO, WeBe Life Inc.**

# SELF!SH ™

### STEP INTO A JOURNEY OF SELF-DISCOVERY TO REVIVE CONFIDENCE, JOY, AND MEANING

## STEPHANIE SZOSTAK
#### WITH GIVE AN HOUR

A POST HILL PRESS BOOK
ISBN: 978-1-63758-889-5

Self!sh:
Step Into a Journey of Self-Discovery to Revive Confidence, Joy,
and Meaning
© 2023 by Stephanie Szostak
All Rights Reserved

Cover Art, Design, and Branding by Little Big Brands
Interior Design and Infographics by Riva Fischel

Post Hill Press
New York · Nashville
posthillpress.com

Published in the United States of America
1 2 3 4 5 6 7 8 9 10

**Here's To YOU**

To the wild and the wise within you.

*To feeling safe.*

*To joining the DANCE OF LIFE,*
*and staying AWAKE through it all.*

To remembering the greatest gift
you CAN GIVE YOURSELF

**is always there within you,**

waiting for you to come home to YOURSELF,

and let the light from within

shine inside and out of your wonderFULL being.

# THE SELF!SH GLOSSARY

## MENTAL FITNESS

It's like a gym or yoga studio for your mind. Mental fitness is a proactive approach to well-being that encourages self-awareness and regular self-care practices. By cracking open your Self!sh Playbook every day and getting your mental reps in, you can develop a stronger mental game, even on challenging days.

## SELF!SH

A play on words combining "self" and "ish" to create a positive spin on the word "selfish." It's about taking time for yourself every day, owning it as a good thing, and bringing more of what you cherish and value to the world and those around you. That's Self!sh.

## SELF!SH STRATEGIES

Your personal set of strategies, goals, and principles that align with your values and priorities. Think of it as the blueprint that helps you navigate life's uncertainty. Your Self!sh strategies will include examples of successful outcomes, joyful moments, and reminders of all that helps you heal, grow, and thrive.

## SELF!SH PLAYBOOK

Just like sports teams and businesses have playbooks, you've got your own personal playbook for life. It's your tool kit to cope and grow. It's unique to you. It gets you back to the best of you.

## MIND SHIFT

It's like hitting the reset button on your perspective. A mind shift is a change in perspective that allows you to approach a situation in a new or different way. Your Self!sh Playbook serves as a tool to shift your mental game and remind you of the strategies that help get you back on track.

## DAILY MENTAL PREP

The act of preparing yourself mentally and emotionally for the day ahead. It's like putting on your mental armor. Kick start the day with intention and direction, so that you are better prepared to handle whatever comes your way.

## TO DO A 180

The act of turning to your Self!sh Playbook for guidance and support. As a daily mental prep, or whenever you need a mind shift, take three minutes—180 seconds— to do a 180 on your frame of mind. Open your Playbook on your phone, pick your soundtrack, hit PLAY and let it give your heart, mind, and soul the boost they need.

## MENTAL GAME

The mindset and approach you bring to any given situation or challenge. It involves the ability to manage your thoughts, emotions and behaviors. A strong mental game can help stay focused, respond versus react, and be adaptable in the face of adversity.

# FOREWORD

## BY JOHN O'LEARY

**ONE KNOCK ON THE DOOR CHANGED MY LIFE.**

Although it seemed at first to be changed for the worse, the person who showed up, the lessons she taught, and the mind shift that occurred undoubtedly changed my life.

After being burned on 100 percent of my body at age nine, I was given very little chance of surviving. Five months in the hospital, dozens of surgeries, and innumerable procedures later, the little boy who was expected to die was liberated to go home with his family and return to life.

There were major problems though.

I was at home because it was impossible for me to go back to school. I was in a wheelchair because my legs were still too weak to support my weight. I was unable to do anything for myself because my fingers had been amputated. And, more than the physical struggles, even as a young boy I knew there would be little for me in this life ahead. I had survived a fire, yes, but what kind of life was this?

And then there was that knock on the door.

My mother greeted the guest and ushered her into the house. Mom approached my wheelchair, bent down, and released the brakes. She reversed my wheelchair away from the kitchen table and pushed me down the hallway into our family room.

"Mom, where are you taking me?"

Instead of answering, Mom pushed me away from the spot where I'd been stuck in the kitchen and moved me toward a new destination, a new perspective, a new mindset.

She rolled me to the piano, relatched the brakes, and calmly told the guest—Mrs. Bartello, the piano teacher—she'd be in the kitchen if we needed anything.

Now stranded alone with Mrs. Bartello, she put her arm around me and shared that although this would be difficult, we could do it together. The teacher then took out a pencil and a rubber band from her purse, wrapped the rubber band around my right hand, binding the pencil to the end of my bandages. With this single pencil protruding from my right hand, Mrs. Bartello instructed me to begin playing the notes on that sheet of paper.

What followed was the longest thirty minutes of my life.

As I listlessly hit the piano keys with the pencil, I remember distinctly thinking, *I hate my mom.*

I could not believe she was making me take piano lessons in the condition I was in. The only good that came out of it was that the lesson ended eventually. At least I'd never have to do that again.

Tragically, the following Tuesday, there was another knock on the front door. Mrs. Bartello came back. And a knock the following Tuesday. For five years of Tuesdays!

Gradually, painfully, begrudgingly, note by note, a bewildered boy with no fingers, with ostensibly no chance of returning to life as it once was, learned to play the piano. First with a single pencil bound to the bandage on his right hand. Then one bound to his left. As the wrappings were removed, I learned to play with the tips of my knuckles and by rolling my palm, creating makeshift chords with the parts of my hands that remained.

Looking back on those Tuesdays, I realize that Mrs. Bartello and my mom weren't simply teaching me the piano. They had no expectations that I'd perform at a recital or enter any competitions.

They were developing something more important than musical ability.

By releasing the brakes on my wheelchair and pushing me toward a goal that seemed unattainable, by seeing potential and hope where any reasonable person would see only disability and despair, they delivered a message—without speaking a word—that I needed to hear and heed.

Today I am fortunate to host a podcast, be the author of two national bestselling books, and travel the world as a speaker. I am a husband and father of four, and I feel extremely fortunate every day of life.

> THROUGH HER LESSONS SHE REVEALED THAT THINGS WILL LIKELY BE DIFFERENT THAN WE HAD PLANNED, BUT IN TIME AND WITH EFFORT, THINGS WILL BE BETTER THAN WE COULD EVEN IMAGINE.

A knock on the door decades earlier was the wakeup call I needed to become aware of what was possible in my life. A teacher showed up to remind me that regardless of the challenges I faced—or might face in the future—I possessed the agency to do what seemed impossible at first. Through her lessons she revealed that things will likely be different than we had planned, but in time and with effort, things will be better than we could even imagine.

My friends, that was a vital message that I needed to hear as a young boy struggling with uncertainty and self-doubt, facing overwhelming physical challenges and limiting beliefs.

It's a powerful message the world needs to receive today.

And it's a lesson Stephanie Szostak has applied throughout her entire life and shares luminously in this workbook.

I have had the honor of calling Stephanie a friend for years. She's a brilliant, beautiful, and accomplished actor. Her journey in life has rarely been easy though. From her upbringing in France to her courageous journey to the United States; from her experiences playing golf at the college level to her unbelievably successful midlife shift into a career as an actor to her ability to still cherish and embrace her most important role as the matriarch of a growing family, Stephanie has modeled grit, drive, and humility. She's also one of the most joyful individuals I know.

She now shares the how-tos of creating a Playbook that will stoke within you possibility, clarity of focus, and self-empowerment to harness the best of your life—not only a guide for the successive chapters of your life but also a repository for future insight gathered along the way.

You are about to be reminded that although you can't always choose the path you walk in life, you are free to determine the manner in which you walk it. You are about to rediscover the gift of being in love with life and confident that better days remain ahead. You are about to begin a journey—your Self!sh journey—that reinforces the grandeur of your life and your ability to determine what happens next in your story.

Be engaged as you go through this book.

> YOU ARE ABOUT TO BE REMINDED
> THAT ALTHOUGH YOU CAN'T ALWAYS
> CHOOSE THE PATH YOU WALK IN LIFE,
> YOU ARE FREE TO DETERMINE THE
> MANNER IN WHICH YOU WALK IT.

Not so much because of the accomplishments of Stephanie or the wisdom imparted by those she references throughout these pages, but in the fact that she is ultimately holding up a mirror reminding you of the priceless worth of your life, the gifts you possess, and the truth that the best of your journey remains ahead.

My friends, consider this book the knock on *your* door.

Consider Stephanie the friend who puts her arm around you, reminding you that life might sometimes be difficult, but we can do it together.

And consider this the Playbook that not only helps positively shift your mindset, but ultimately reveals a magnificent life awaiting to be lived. Starting now.

## JOHN O'LEARY

National bestselling author of the books *On Fire* and *In Awe*

# PREFACE

**I AM NOT A MENTAL HEALTH PROFESSIONAL.**

Heck, I've never even played one on TV. As an actress, I tend to get cast as the adulteress—blame it on the French accent. **But, I have partnered with Give an Hour**, and together we are bringing you this guide. Within these pages, you will find some of the strategies that have helped me achieve the greatest makeover of my life—a mindset makeover.

> **GIVE AN HOUR**, a national mental health nonprofit organization, envisions a world where everyone understands the importance of their mental health and has access to quality care. They provide direct counseling, peer support groups, and educational services to those in need, and empower communities and individuals to develop the skills that will allow them to better care for themselves and those they love.

In 2018, while filming the ABC series *A Million Little Things* (and yes, I happened to be playing an adulteress!), I was introduced to Give an Hour's founder, Dr. Barbara Van Dahlen, who served as a mental health consultant to the show. As you may know, the show explored the reality of mental health and illness, highlighting how family and friends often struggle to share or express their emotional pain openly. Dr. Van Dahlen and I had the most engaging conversations on set, which led to a delightful lunch in NYC and later to me becoming a Give an Hour Ambassador.

In 2021, in the middle of the pandemic, Give an Hour and I collaborated on a four-part webinar series focused on the importance of cultivating a healthy mindset and encouraging people to create a personal Playbook—a tool I developed to prevent valuable insights and guidance from getting lost in notebooks, on my phone, laptop, or, worse, completely forgotten. My personal Playbook helped me consolidate and integrate knowledge, while also improving my self-esteem in a career (acting) that surely does wonders for one's confidence (not!).

The feedback was consistently positive but the one question that kept coming up was "What do I put in my Playbook?!" "That's personal," I'd say, "whatever it is that connects you to you, that helps you connect to others and the world around you better." Not a very tangible guideline, I admit.

After watching the webinars, an entrepreneur from my hometown reached out asking if we could develop a workbook that could serve as a starting point for people to create their playbook. We loved the idea, got to work, and here it is!

## A FEW WORDS FROM DR. TRINA CLAYEUX, CEO OF GIVE AN HOUR:

Imagine waking up each and every morning with a tool that brings you to a more peaceful and thoughtful place. Maybe you're in your favorite comfy clothes and sipping that first sip of coffee. No texts, no emails, no news.... Just quiet time for you to get reinspired, centered, and reminded of how you want to show up in the world on this day. How different do you think you would then feel?

The annual national survey conducted by the American Psychological Association (APA) reports that we are "a battered American psyche, facing a barrage of external stressors that are mostly out of personal control." No matter who we are, we all get impacted and stressed by external factors and circumstances. APA's chief executive officer, Arthur C. Evans Jr., reminds us that "focusing on accomplishing goals that are in our control can help prevent our minds from getting overwhelmed by the many uncertainties in life."

The Self!sh workbook will help you gain focus on what you can control—one of the exercises specifically helps you identify daily goals that are in your control—but beyond goals, taking time to check-in with yourself and review your Playbook on a daily basis will place your focus and attention on the beliefs, practices, and skills that help you cope, respond, and thrive in the face of adversity. **By reminding yourself of your preferred supportive thoughts and actions, you can disrupt negative thinking and begin your day feeling inspired and empowered**. I've completed my own Playbook and can testify to its benefits through consistent use. A small daily dose of mental fitness goes a long way to building mental health and emotional well-being.

# INTRO

> **"**
>
> "When the student is ready the teacher will appear.
> When the student is truly ready....
> The teacher will disappear."
>
> —*TAO TE CHING*

## A LITTLE BIT ABOUT ME

Growing up, two of my most significant *teachers* were my dad and my brother. My dad taught me that the quality of my thoughts affected my performance—in life and, most importantly, on the golf course. "One shot at a time," he'd remind me again and again to keep me focused on the present moment. My older brother didn't give two turds about golf. He was a Rastafari, and a rebel. He taught me to be independent-minded and to not follow the herd. He questioned everything and saw the world in unique ways. He also made me aware at a very young age of the complexities of the human mind, as I saw him struggling to fit in and battle his heroin addiction. He died much too young at twenty-eight years old, and he continues to inspire me every day.

## FASCINATED BY THE MIND

I wanted to be a social worker when I started college, to help kids like my brother. But instead, I did the more practical and predictable thing: studied business and graduated with a marketing degree. I landed in fabulous NYC, in the glamorous world of fashion at Chanel—this corporate cubical stint wasn't quite the right fit for me BUT it ended up being a great dry run for what was on the horizon. At the age of twenty-nine, I followed a quiet but persistent inner voice and signed up for my first-ever acting class. It was a theater studio in New York City and it was serious work. There were working actors and students. Twice a week, I'd watch them put up scenes of plays I'd never heard of and slip in and out of themselves. They made it seem so simple, so natural. The playfulness, the physicality, the freedom, the pain, the exploration, I was blown away by it all. It took me weeks to get my butt off my chair and get on stage and when I finally did, I lasted no more than a minute. "Stop!" my teacher bellowed, "I don't believe a word you're saying!" She sent my scene partner back to his seat and laid into me for what seemed to be an eternity. She crushed me. The audacity I had thinking I was ready to work, thinking I could waltz myself into "acting" just because I wanted to. The disregard I had for the craft. The incapacity I had at standing on my two feet. The permanent smile on my face—"Is what I'm saying funny to you?" she asked. I shook my head no. She humiliated me. She pissed me off. She hurt me. But she woke me up to my pretending, to a part of myself I had buried deep inside of me. I knew I had to do this. I knew I had found my passion (and my teacher!). So, I didn't become a social worker. I only "play pretend" for a living, but still, as an actress I get to dig into the psyche of characters, even if only fictional, and try to understand why they do the things they do and think the things they think. Why do they get in their own way and not necessarily do what serves them best? How ironic is it then that a decade after I started my acting career, after making my way from independent movies to playing Jacqueline Follet opposite Meryl Streep in *The Devil Wears Prada*, I had to dig into *my own psyche* and figure out *why my mind* was undermining my confidence, my joy, and my well-being?

## LOSING MY WAY

"That sucked. They're gonna think it sucked. They're gonna think *I* suck. I do suck. What am I doing here? I don't belong here. I'm gonna get fired." That was my inner dialogue on the set of my first lead role in a major studio film, *Dinner for Schmucks*. I was flooded with self-doubt. My inner dialogue was toxic. I felt like an outsider. Like a complete beginner. I lost my way. There I was, being handed the opportunity to work with comedic icons Paul Rudd and Steve Carell, and I lost my ability to trust, play, and let go. I completely lost my confidence and I didn't have the tools to shake off the mental chatter and recalibrate.

## LEARNING NEW WAYS

My mother told me that her forties were her best decade. She said that, for her, it was when she finally knew who she was and didn't care what other people thought. Well, I was forty and I was longing for a whole lot of that. I had some learning to do and began DIGGING into books, podcasts, and online courses. I incorporated new daily rituals into my life that worked for me—gratitude, meditation, and journaling. I learned new skills that helped me not only with my confidence and mental health but also gave me a new outlook on life—a new sense of purpose and meaning—that was bigger than my career and bigger than me. I got a clearer idea of what kind of life I wanted to live and who I was. I got a *Mindset makeover*....

"The privilege of a lifetime is being who you are."

—*JOSEPH CAMPBELL*

## BUT THE CHALLENGE REMAINED....

How would I remember all this guidance? How could I give it staying power? I heard the psychologist and grit expert, Angela Duckworth, explain on the *Finding Mastery* podcast how she can "help people make plans to change and make differences in their lives but—Why doesn't it stick? Why isn't it accumulating?" ***That*** **is precisely the WHY behind The Self!sh Playbook.**

## WHY A PLAYBOOK?

On any given day, our frame of mind and mental game has the power to determine how we feel and respond to the world. There isn't much we're in control of in our lives. We're not in control of outcomes, what other people think or what they do, or even the random thoughts that pop in and out of our own awareness. But what we *do* have control over is how we *respond.* Just as sports teams and businesses have playbooks with the set of strategies and plays to help them stay focused, adapt, and respond to challenges, why don't we have a playbook for our own lives?

## TAKING OFF FOR THE DAY

Have you ever stepped on an airplane and caught a glimpse of the pilot going over their checklist in the cockpit? Even though pilots have all flown thousands of hours, been assigned the same route again and again, their process is the same each time—they check all the instruments, the flight plan, the fuel, the weather, prepare for turbulence, and get ready for takeoff. It doesn't matter how much training they have, how great their skills are, or how much experience they have, the checklist is a requisite. Now, there are a lot of other planes on the tarmac. What if instead, our pilot got distracted listening in on the planes next to it in the taxi line. "Oh nice—that one is going to the Bahamas. Wow. I bet they have great weather there. It's a short flight. That *would* be nice." Next thing you know, it's their turn to zoom down the runway and take off. How dangerous would it be if the pilot skipped the checklist and instead got sidetracked by the other planes?

**Yet that is what we do most mornings. We get sidetracked.**

IN 1860, RALPH WALDO EMERSON SAID:

> 66
>
> "He who should inspire and lead his race must be defended from traveling with the souls of other men, from living, breathing, reading, and writing in the daily, time-worn yoke of their opinions."

HOWEVER, IN TODAY'S WORLD, WE OFTEN END UP AMPLI-FYING ALL THE NOISE THAT'S DRILLING DOWN ON US LIKE A MADDENING WOODPECKER.

## HOW DOES THIS HAPPEN?

From the second we wake up, thoughts pop into our head—how did we sleep, our body's aches and pains, the to-do list of the day. Then we grab our phones and the digital deluge begins—texts, emails, news, social media. People's comments, opinions, and agendas prickle us one way or another, and all of it crepes (wait, that is a French dish) "creeps" into our psyche, tainting the window through which we see the world. Our attention gets hijacked (like a pilot skipping their checklist) by the busyness of our modern lives and the ever-present technology.

## WHAT DOES THIS LEAD TO?

Drained and busy minds that lead us astray. Easily caught up in other people's opinions, wishing and wanting things to be different, revving up frustration, fear, doubt, anger, anxiety, blame, comparison, and an "us vs. them" mentality. **It affects our peace of mind, our emotional well-being, our relationships, our productivity, and our sleep.**

## HOW IS THIS SERVING US?

We are getting really good at being distracted, moving away from good judgment, what we're working towards, and what serves us well. This is the information age and we are experiencing information overload. We often lose steam, run on autopilot, and, as we face the challenges and obstacles of the day, we don't always *respond* in the best way.

## WHAT IF INSTEAD WE HAD A CHECKLIST JUST LIKE OUR PILOT?

A checklist to remind us of our own flight path, get us ready for take-off each day, and prepare us for the inevitable turbulences. Enter *Self!sh*, your personal Playbook for your mindset, with everything that brings you joy, purpose, and meaning, and points you back to your North Star.

The *Self!sh* Playbook is a 180-degree shift from the routines and habits that are disconnecting and distracting us from our flight path in life.

> IT IS NOT SOCIAL MEDIA; IT IS THE OPPOSITE. IT IS PERSONAL, PRIVATE MEDIA.

It is a connection to YOU for yourSELF so that you get to bring more of what you cherish and value to life and those around you.

## HOW WILL IT DO THIS?

Start your day on the right foot by viewing your Playbook so that, before you subject yourself to the outside stressors of the world, you are reminded of all that encourages, inspires, and motivates you—everything that helps YOU heal, grow, and thrive. Load it all up in the forefront of your mind before the woodpecker has a chance to start banging on your temple.

## WHAT MIGHT IT LEAD TO?

Clarity and peace versus chaos and conflict. Shift your attention and fuel your heart, mind, and soul with carefully chosen words, wisdom, and imagery. Rev up compassion, courage, and confidence. **Reinforce the *Self!sh Strategies* that *connect you to the best of who you are* and bring about a *more skillful version of yourself.***

## HOW COULD IT SERVE US?

All of your insight and guidance is in a central location and is easily retrievable so that you can revisit it and benefit from it again and again. Going over your Playbook every day is like doing reps at the gym—except these reps aren't for physical fitness, they're for mental fitness. The more consistent your reps are, the more your good thoughts will be top of mind and turn into habitual thoughts—like "brain muscle memory"—and the better prepared you will be to respond (vs. react) to the challenges of the day. Never perfect. Just better because *what we practice, we become.*

**"**

"If you feed your mind as often as you feed your stomach,

then you'll never have to worry about feeding your stomach

or having a roof over your head or clothes on your back."

—*ALBERT EINSTEIN*

*WHAT ARE YOUR*

## SELF!SH STRATEGIES?

The set of beliefs, principles and skills that are beneficial to YOU.

All that empowers you to be YOU and connects you to the best of who you are.

The "good thoughts" that help you quiet down the noise, the doubt, and the critic.

# WHAT TO EXPECT?

This workbook is built around these eight self-reflection exercises.

We will guide you every step of the way through prompts, questions, and examples that will lead you to creating YOUR own PLAYBOOK.

I didn't make up these exercises; they are versions of simple yet creative questions I answered while working with coaches, mentors, and therapists over the years. What I discovered answering some of these questions continues to guide me to this day. I hope you will find them pertinent and that they will help you make discoveries of your own.

**Each exercise will have:**

- A story from a Give an Hour ambassador
- An exercise with open space for you to write in and brainstorm
- The Why, including exercise benefits and the science behind it
- Examples for your Playbook entry
- A brain dump section for extra writing space

## PART TWO
## YOUR SELF!SH PLAYBOOK

Answers to the exercises will feed the content of your Playbook.

Decide if you'd prefer to have your Playbook on your **phone** or in a **notebook**.

I created mine on my phone as an album in my photos. The advantages are that it's with me at all times, I can scroll through it if I need a mind shift, play it as a slideshow with music, and it's easier to edit, add to it, or archive stuff I don't need anymore. An artist I spoke to said she'd create hers in a notebook with sketches and illustrations, and then take screenshots of those to have a digital version as well.

**MAKE YOUR PLAYBOOK LOOK GOOD (FOR YOU).** The more you like the way it looks, the better it will make you feel, and the more you'll want to revisit it. Research shows that mixing emotionally appealing visuals, words, and music together helps stimulate attention, boost mood, motivation, and our ability to learn and remember.

**CONNECT TEXT WITH IMAGERY.** Pair your text entries with compelling pictures, graphics, or artwork! Combining words with meaningful imagery evokes our emotional centers and helps embed what we want to remember into our long-term memory.

For example, if you write an affirmation such as: "I am prepared, I work hard," find a visual that symbolizes that for you—it could be a picture of you in action doing something difficult, such as training for a marathon. Not that you should train for a marathon. I've never trained for a marathon. And I never will.

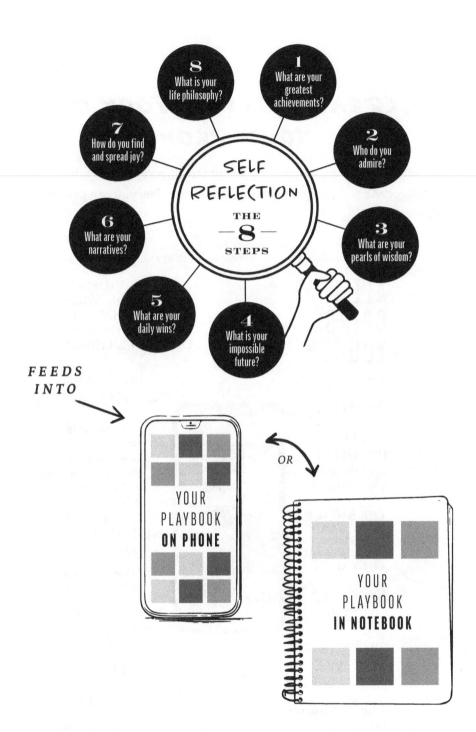

# CREATING A PLAYBOOK ON YOUR PHONE

Create a dedicated album in your photo library specifically for your Playbook. **As you progress through each exercise, you can decide what content to add.**

> Select the slideshow option and watch all your reminders come to life on your phone with the music of your choice.

## ALL THAT BRINGS YOU JOY

*What you're grateful for*

The people that lift you up when you're down

THE ADVICE FROM YOUR MENTORS, COACHES OR THERAPISTS

The skills you want to sharpen

THE GOALS YOU ARE AIMING FOR

The inspirational figures in your life

## HARD EVIDENCE FROM YOUR LIFE THAT YOU CAN HANDLE DIFFICULT THINGS

The values you want to live by

*The wisdom that keeps you motivated and encourages you to forge ahead*

## YOUR HOPES AND DREAMS

All that helps you quiet the noise, the doubt, the critic, and will connect you to the best of who you are

## ALL THAT EMPOWERS YOU TO BE YOU

My Playbook is filled with pictures, screenshots, and entries I created with the free apps Quotes Creator and Canva. Both apps have great designs you can customize with your own pictures and text. I'm also excited to announce that we're currently working on developing the Self!sh app, which will serve as a home for your Playbook. The app is designed to provide a convenient and user-friendly platform to help you create and get the most out of your Self!sh Playbook. We're hoping to launch the app soon, so stay tuned for updates! We can't wait to share it with you and help you take your Self!sh journey to the next level.

❝

"Research suggests that when we see ourselves clearly, we are more confident and more creative. We make sounder decisions, build stronger relationships, and communicate more effectively. We're less likely to lie, cheat, and steal. We are better workers who get more promotions. And we're more effective leaders with more satisfied employees and more profitable companies."

—*TASHA EURICH, psychologist*

Watch her TED Talk "Increase your self-awareness with one simple fix."

Photo by Elena Seibert

# PLAYBOOK BENEFITS

## 1 — DIRECTION

Goals

Strengths

Life Philosophy

Values

Vision

## 2 — CONFIDENCE

Achievements

Lessons learned

Self-Talk

Skills you're working on

## 3 — JOY

All the good in your life

Memories

What brings you joy

How you spread joy

## 4 — GUIDANCE

Support from friends and family

Wisdom from therapy, coaches, mentors, support groups, spiritual leaders, and people you admire

---

*BETTER* **THINKING** → *BETTER* **FEELING** → *BETTER* **DOING**

---

# BENEFITS FROM COMPLETING THIS WORKBOOK

1. A deeper understanding of who you are and what your values are.

2. Clarity on the kind of life you want to live, and the steps you can take to get there.

3. Your very own Self!sh Playbook:

   - A comprehensive, dynamic, and ever-evolving mental fitness tool to stay focused on your unique journey and prioritize your needs, goals, and values.

   - A daily mental prep practice to start each day **with direction and intention, reinforce good thinking**, and **enhance overall well-being**.

   - Easily accessible, you can refer to it whenever you need a mind shift, to prepare for a big event, or to navigate a tough conversation. While it's not a cure-all, your Playbook provides a framework to fall back on: to **Pause, quiet down the noise, shift your focus to what serves you well, and reconnect to the best of who you are**.

# THE STAGE IS YOURS

## WRITE FOR YOURSELF ONLY

Write with honesty. Consider this your invitation to pull the mask away, forget the roles you play, the job title, or the status symbol. Take a journey inward with humility and compassion. Surrender. Make space for all of you, the bold and the vulnerable.

This isn't about proving anything to yourself or anyone else. There is no audience here. This is about getting acquainted with the mysterious within. Surprise yourself! We all have our own story to live. Explore what that means for you. Quiet down your inner critic. Follow your heart. Find your voice. Jump in feet first!

❧ Once you begin an exercise, try not to peek ahead. That'd be like skipping to the last page of a murder mystery—you might ruin the big reveal if you read ahead, so take it one step at a time and savor the process.

## TAKE THE LEAD

This is your guide. Start with what inspires you. Feel free to jump around. Go at your own pace. The magic happens if you take what's here and make it your own. See what resonates, keep what works, and toss what doesn't fit for YOU. We suggest you end with Step Eight only because completing the earlier exercises might help you with this final one. But again, this is your workbook, you decide.

**❝**

"When you ask the question, 'Who am I?'

If you have enough time and concentration,

you may find some surprising answers."

*—THICH NHAT HANH*

**TAKE A JOURNEY INWARD WITH HUMILITY AND COMPASSION.**

♛ And the Self!sh Playbook default is PRIVATE! (Does anyone else think it's weird that Venmo's default option is PUBLIC? So anyone on the platform can see who you are sending money to?!)

**STEP**

**1**

# WHAT ARE YOUR GREATEST ACHIEVEMENTS?

66 The greatest accomplishment
is not in never falling, but in
**rising again after you fall.** 99

—*VINCE LOMBARDI*

*STORY BY*

## SHOWTIME SHAWN PORTER

Former two-time welterweight world champion, podcast host, and Give an Hour Ambassador

---

# THE YEAR IS 2018.

My dad is my coach, in life and in the ring. He is demanding and tough, and he is old-school. His philosophy is to "break you down to build you back up." And that coaching style is not working for me anymore. I've been training my whole life, fighting my way to the top, and now I'm finally ready, waiting for my shot at the World Boxing Council (WBC) World Welterweight Title. "Waiting" because in boxing—unlike in any other sports—there is no set schedule and there is no telling when or even if you'll ever get your chance at fighting for the belt.

One day, out of frustration, I went to play basketball, something my father would definitely not approve of, and...of course, I get hurt. As I'm debating how to tell him, my phone rings and he's calling with the news we've been waiting for. We are invited to challenge for the WBC World Welterweight Title in New York City.

> EVERYTHING I HAVE WORKED TOWARDS AND DREAMED OF IS NOW ON THE LINE.

I come clean to my dad. He's mad. He doubts I can be ready for the fight, but after much convincing on my part, he agrees to move forward. We decide to keep the injury to ourselves. My dad handles the business side of things and the fight is set. I now need to get healthy.

We forged on as our relationship worsened. We're both blaming each other for anything that goes wrong. We are constantly fighting and arguing in the gym. Outside the gym, our relationship is nonexistent.

Finally, we agree to bring in a new coach to train me. And then I completely shut off my dad. This wasn't the first time, but definitely the time with the most at stake. As the fight gets closer, I shut off everyone. I don't allow anyone to enter my emotional space. It was my way of protecting myself, controlling and sealing my emotions. I thought if I spoke, people would try to fix things and it would unlock those emotions and that was not what I needed to do to get ready to step into the ring and become the WBC World Champion.

Game time.

Barclays Center in Brooklyn, New York, against Danny Garcia. I'm about to go into the ring. My dad and I are still not speaking. We didn't fly to NYC together. We didn't see each other in the hotel. This is the biggest fight of my career and I'm about to go into the ring and in that moment—even though we haven't spoken in months—all of a sudden, I find my forehead pressed against my dad's and slowly, we start to sway. Slowly, we fall back into our ritual. Like two wild rams gearing up for battle. People always thought we were praying but we weren't, it was just some ritual that we developed over the years. And that night without thinking, when we stepped into the ring, the moment we needed to be teammates, the moment we needed to be father and son to achieve the mission of greatness, we locked heads.

The bell rings, and we do what we've always done. In between rounds, he gives me instructions; I go back out and fight and

> WE KNOW WE STILL HAVE TO DO THE HARD THINGS TO KEEP OUR RELATIONSHIP HEALTHY, ONLY NOW WE DON'T DO IT FOR THE BELT, WE DO IT FOR THE NEXT GENERATION.

come back into the corner and do it again. Halfway through the fight, my dad gives me a look that says, we got this. Not something he usually does. I'm not convinced since Garcia is on home turf and undefeated in NYC. I keep on fighting. And it isn't until the referee grabs my hand and raises my arm to signify the winner that I realize: we have done it.

We went home Champions. Professionally and personally.

Nothing about those months with my dad—the frustration, the anger, the pain, and the silence—was ideal. Yet, all those elements served a purpose that not only led us to the welterweight title but also led us to mending things. We both grew from this experience. We did some maturing. We became better teammates, better father and son, better coach and athlete. And we know we still have to do the hard things to keep our relationship healthy, only now we don't do it for the Belt, we do it for the next generation.

# STEP 1

## WHAT ARE YOUR GREATEST ACHIEVEMENTS?

Achievements can be the *wins and successes* but also the *hard moments* when you fell, failed, and then got back up. Moments when you felt like you were sucker punched and at the time you did not think you would be able to get up off the mat but you found a way. They can be instances when you helped others or had the courage to ask for help. Your greatest achievements probably took guts, determination, strength, and hard work, and most likely involved pain, vulnerability, and love.

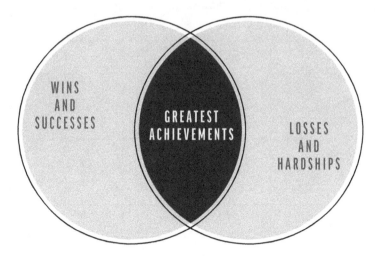

WINS AND SUCCESSES

GREATEST ACHIEVEMENTS

LOSSES AND HARDSHIPS

# SELF!SH

**1** Write down five to ten (or more) of these moments for you.

**MAKE A LIST**

---

_____

_____

_____

_____

_____

_____

_____

_____

_____

_____

_____

_____

_____

_____

_____

_____

_____

_____

_____

# STEP 1

 Once you've made your list, go back to the top and one by one, allow your mind and emotions to take you back to these moments. Ask yourself:

- What was it that got me through this? What did it take for me to make it through?
- Who were the people that helped me or those I might have helped along the way?

_____

_____

_____

_____

_____

_____

_____

_____

_____

_____

_____

_____

_____

_____

_____

What are some of the character strengths and qualities you embodied to achieve these outcomes? Use your own words or you can refer to the VIA list on the right.

_____

_____

_____

_____

_____

_____

_____

_____

_____

_____

_____

_____

_____

_____

_____

_____

_____

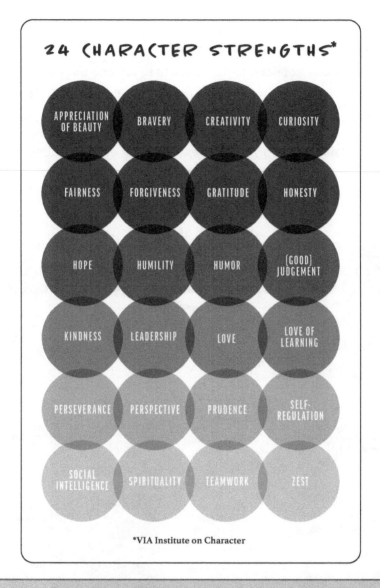

# 24 CHARACTER STRENGTHS*

| | | | |
|---|---|---|---|
| APPRECIATION OF BEAUTY | BRAVERY | CREATIVITY | CURIOSITY |
| FAIRNESS | FORGIVENESS | GRATITUDE | HONESTY |
| HOPE | HUMILITY | HUMOR | (GOOD) JUDGEMENT |
| KINDNESS | LEADERSHIP | LOVE | LOVE OF LEARNING |
| PERSEVERANCE | PERSPECTIVE | PRUDENCE | SELF-REGULATION |
| SOCIAL INTELLIGENCE | SPIRITUALITY | TEAMWORK | ZEST |

*VIA Institute on Character

**NOTE:** Did you know that the VIA Institute has identified twenty-four character strengths and that we all possess them, just in different unique proportions? If you want to learn more about your top strengths, head on over to https://www.viacharacter.org to take the free in-depth test. It only takes about fifteen minutes to identify and discover how to harness the power of your strengths.

**4** Sum up each of your achievements in one or two words. This word does not need to make sense to anyone but you. It can be an adjective or a name—any word really. The point is that this word will emotionally connect you to that experience.

The table below gives a few examples for each question.

## GREATEST ACHIEVEMENTS
*(examples)*

| | STEP 1 Achievements | STEP 2 What got you there? | STEP 3 One word | STEP 4 Play Book Visual |
|---|---|---|---|---|
| Example 1 | Back to college on my own, graduating at 27 | Perseverance through the tough times. Pushed myself. Not afraid to take a risk. Hard work. Asking for help and support. My mentor. | MADISON | "I did this on my own, my own way" written over my graduation picture. |
| Example 2 | Rehab, all in, meetings, got help, support, getting myself back together | Courage to change my life, honesty with myself and others, support from AA, doctor, family. Not being afraid to be vulnerable. | PEACE | Picture of Sobriety Coin |
| Example 3 | Mom, there for her through last year | Compassion, love, John helping out | MAMA | Picture of us at the fair |
| Example 4 | Supporting my family | Adapting, working hard. Opening up. Doctor J. Discipline! | NEVER QUIT | Picture of the 4 of us |

You get the picture....

**Now write your own.**

# STEP 1

# THE WHY

## EXERCISE BENEFIT

Through this exercise you will identify how far you've come, what you've accomplished, what you've survived, and the lives you've touched. These moments are hard evidence that YOU can do difficult things. Leadership coach Jay Wang of Southwestern Consulting says this exercise is "the meat and potatoes behind your achievements. It serves not only as a tangible reminder of what you've accomplished but also showcases the character strengths that you do in fact exhibit."

## THE SCIENCE BEHIND IT

Studies have shown that looking back on past achievements and accomplishments can help us reframe our perspective, increase our sense of accomplishment, boost confidence, build meaning and purpose, and contribute to developing positive well-being. Additionally, focusing on personal strengths and support systems can lead to developing a more positive and resilient mindset, which can help us cope with challenges more effectively.

## PLAYBOOK ENTRY EXAMPLES
### (do what works for you!):

- Use a list or pictures to illustrate your Greatest Achievements.

- Add your one word, your character strengths, and/or an affirmation such as "I can do hard things." Make it your own, make it fun, and use your own words!

- Add the strategies that got you there. Make them a part of your resilience toolkit.

- Remember: your Playbook is PRIVATE. Don't worry about what someone else may think. No one will see this. Don't censor yourself. Do YOU.

I can do hard 💩
I've done this... I'm doing this
1. Life after Divorce
2. Meeting Dan and trusting him, with my HEART
3. Raised two girls, LOVE
4. Back to work
5. RUNNING again!

**MY HIGHLIGHTS**
- AA all in
- Our girls, Lisa being there for them
- Honest with them
- My business, going after it year after year

NYC MARATHON

# STEP 1

## BRAIN DUMP

---
---
---
---
---
---
---
---
---
---
---
---
---
---
---
---
---
---
---
---

# STEP 1

---

 

# SELF!SH

_____

_____

_____

_____

_____

_____

_____

_____

_____

_____

_____

_____

_____

_____

_____

_____

_____

_____

_____

_____

_____

_____

_____

# STEP 1

## STEP
## 2

# WHO DO YOU
# ADMIRE?

> " Knowing what you admire in
> others is a **wonderful mirror** into
> your deepest, as yet unborn, self. "

—*GRETCHEN RUBIN*

*STORY BY*

## BOB STEAD

Army combat medic, veteran, licensed counselor, and
Give an Hour Ambassador

### WHAT I FOUND MOST INTERESTING

about this exercise was that I already had the answers and potentially could have been living from that expression for thirty years if I had paid attention to myself. Mindfulness is about being in tune with your own energy, your own skill set, and your own measure of identity. I do not think it is enough for us to simply say we admire this person or that person from a big picture.

Using this exercise, I was able to zero in on not only what I admired about so many people that have crossed my path, but also *why*. This presents an opportunity for me to not only acknowledge those who have come before me, but also emulate those characteristics that made those people such a powerful force in my life.

Growing up in Chicago, my best friend was Joseph Crockett. Joe had a rough start early in life. He was diagnosed with kidney failure in his teenage years. Joe had dialysis regularly and fought through his illness for years. I never saw Joe frown; I never saw Joe withhold anything from anyone. At one point I was homeless as a teen, and Joe was always by my side, supporting me through my pain while never showing his own. Joe eventually got a transplant in his early twenties. It lasted a year, and his body rejected the transplant. I saw Joe a day before he passed, and I remember it vividly. He was in the hospital hoping for a miracle. He held my hand and said, "I'm scared brother, but it's gonna be okay."

Joe left this world far too early, he was only twenty-three, I think I was twenty-two. It was and still is the most devastating loss I have ever suffered, and I think this exercise really allows me to identify why Joe had such an incredible impact on my life in such a short period compared to a full life. Before completing this exercise, I thought the characteristics that truly made Joe special were sometimes so far out of reach for me. For years, I did not think much of myself; I was raised to believe I wasn't worth much.

I NOW TRY TO LIVE MY LIFE WITH OPTIMISM, COURAGE, AND COMPASSION IN HONOR OF MY FRIEND.

I now try to live my life with optimism, courage, and compassion in honor of my friend. Joe was never selfish, he was never standing with his hand out, and he always looked for ways to support the people in his life. Joe had every right to give up. He didn't deserve to suffer for so long, but to see him in the street you would never know, he would never flinch. *That* is the strength that matters—strength of character, strength of conviction—and *that* is who I want to be.

If you take anything away from this exercise, it is that we must define why and how someone impacts our life in a positive way. It's not enough to simply say something was positive or helpful. Defining the person behind the action we admire allows us to identify a target for our growth. If anything, I learned that before crossing paths with some of these amazing people, I probably could not define what traits are significant to me. It was through the demonstration and discipline of the people I admired that I learned what it meant to not just exist, but to impact the world in any way you can. It may be your name that is invoked in an exercise one day. What a testament to character that would be.

> WE MUST DEFINE WHY AND HOW SOMEONE IMPACTS OUR LIFE IN A POSITIVE WAY. IT'S NOT ENOUGH TO SIMPLY SAY SOMETHING WAS POSITIVE OR HELPFUL.

# STEP 2

# WHO DO YOU ADMIRE?

Who in your life has been a source of inspiration?

 **1** Write down the names of five or more people who inspire you.

- These people can be dead or alive or real or fictional characters.

- Think about family members, friends, characters in your favorite movies or books, a coach or teacher, activists, spiritual leaders, musicians, athletes, writers, artists, poets, etc.

- Brainstorm. But don't think too hard.

### PEOPLE I ADMIRE:

1. _____

2. _____

3. _____

4. _____

5. _____

6. _____

7. _____

8. _____

9. _____

10. _____

After you have your list, ask yourself, "What is it about this person that I really admire? Why do they inspire me? What traits or qualities do they have that I look up to?" Try to come up with three to five characteristics for each person (in case you draw a blank, check out the "Attributes you admire" visual).

QUALITIES I ADMIRE:

_____

_____

_____

_____

_____

_____

_____

_____

_____

_____

_____

_____

_____

_____

## ATTRIBUTES YOU ADMIRE

- ○ Activist
- ○ Advocate
- ○ Artist
- ○ Bold
- ○ Brings People Together
- ○ Clever
- ○ Compassionate
- ○ Confident
- ○ Courageous
- ○ Fighter
- ○ Fights for Others
- ○ Flexible
- ○ Free
- ○ Funny
- ○ Generous
- ○ Hard Working
- ○ Honest
- ○ Humble
- ○ Joyful

- ○ Kind
- ○ Leader
- ○ Light Hearted
- ○ Loving
- ○ Not Afraid of Change
- ○ Open-Minded
- ○ Passionate
- ○ Positive
- ○ Resilient
- ○ Risk Taker
- ○ Selfless
- ○ Serves Others
- ○ Simple
- ○ Smart
- ○ Speaks Up for What's Right
- ○ Truthful
- ○ Visionary
- ○ Warrior
- ○ Wise

Take a look at all the qualities you listed:

- What qualities came up more than once? Circle those and write them in the space below.

- Do you see any qualities with a similar theme? For example, maybe you wrote "funny" for one person and "great sense of humor" for another. Combine similar ones into one trait and pick the one that resonates most with you.

**MOST COMMON QUALITIES**

_____

_____

_____

_____

_____

_____

_____

_____

_____

_____

Did you know that **what we admire and respect in others is often what we desire for ourselves?** It's a fun fact that can reveal a lot about the values you hold most dearly and how YOU strive to show up in life.

# STEP 2

 Looking back at your Greatest Achievements in Step 1, did some of these qualities show up as your character strengths? Would you like to bring more of them to life? What simple daily actions could help you do that?

Use the space below to jot down daily actions that could help you do that.

**EXAMPLE:**

Let's say you want to be more Daring and Authentic in your life. Ask yourself, "How can I do that? How can I shake up my routines and do things differently?" One thing you might come up with is "I will practice being more vulnerable and having more meaningful conversations with people close to me."

**HOW CAN I BRING THESE QUALITIES INTO MY LIFE?**

_____

_____

_____

_____

_____

_____

_____

_____

_____

_____

# THE WHY

## EXERCISE BENEFIT

This exercise expands on the first exercise. It offers a unique approach to discovering the character strengths and core values that are fundamental and unique to who you are. Next time you are feeling stuck or facing a difficult decision, perhaps you can read these characteristics or think of the inspirational figures in your life as a way to reconnect to your priorities and help find the best path forward for you. Remember, these are values and qualities that you already possess. They may be obscured, they may be dormant, but they are in you. No matter what circumstances you're in, expressing yourself through these qualities will align you with your fundamental nature, and help build positive momentum.

## THE SCIENCE BEHIND IT

Admiration is an emotion that not only energizes us physically, it can also stimulate cognitive processes related to motivation. When we admire someone, it can serve as a source of inspiration, motivating us to strive towards our own goals and values. Dr. Steven C. Hayes, founder of Acceptance and Commitment Therapy (ACT), refers to the people we admire as *"Value Guides,"* explaining that *"when you connect with why this person matters to you, you can better bring these qualities into your own life*. In other words, by thinking about your grandma, and why she is important to you, you position yourself to bring the qualities of caring, kindness, loyalty, and resilience into your own life." The process of focusing on the qualities of those we admire, can help us cultivate those same qualities within ourselves, and lead to personal growth and development.

## PLAYBOOK ENTRY EXAMPLES
### (do what works for you!):

- Images of your inspirational figures (combined with the traits you admire).

- A list of the values and character strengths you admire the most.

- Your "how" to practice and honor these traits.

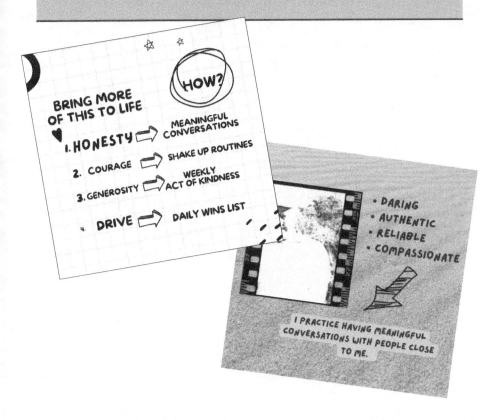

BRING MORE OF THIS TO LIFE — HOW?

1. HONESTY ⟹ MEANINGFUL CONVERSATIONS
2. COURAGE ⟹ SHAKE UP ROUTINES
3. GENEROSITY ⟹ WEEKLY ACT OF KINDNESS
4. DRIVE ⟹ DAILY WINS LIST

- DARING
- AUTHENTIC
- RELIABLE
- COMPASSIONATE

I PRACTICE HAVING MEANINGFUL CONVERSATIONS WITH PEOPLE CLOSE TO ME.

# STEP 2

## BRAIN DUMP

# STEP 2

_____

_____

_____

_____

_____

_____

_____

_____

_____

_____

_____

_____

_____

_____

_____

_____

_____

_____

_____

_____

_____

_____

# SELF!SH

---

---

---

---

---

---

---

---

---

---

---

---

---

---

---

---

---

---

---

---

---

---

---

---

---

# STEP 2

_____

_____

_____

_____

_____

_____

_____

_____

_____

_____

_____

_____

_____

_____

_____

_____

_____

_____

_____

_____

_____

_____

## STEP

# 3

## WHAT ARE YOUR
## PEARLS OF
## WISDOM?

> 66 It takes a wise man to learn from
> his mistakes, but an **even wiser
> man to learn from others.** 99

—*ZEN PROVERB*

## STORY BY

### ELLE MARK

Epidemiologist, Miss Minnesota 2021, and Give an Hour Ambassador

## MY PALMS WERE SWEATING

and I was on the verge of tears as I sat in the front seat of my dad's old Volvo. He took the turn into the middle school parking lot where teachers stood outside ready to welcome us to our first day of sixth grade. I was petrified, and I prayed no one could sense my fear.

As I was picking my backpack up off my feet and preparing to jump out of the car, my dad stopped me. He said, "I know you're afraid, but take a minute today to look around you. There will be someone—maybe sitting alone at lunch or in class—who is struggling more than you. Be a friend to that person."

Now, I should preface that my dad has always been a man of few words. When I would be upset or hurt as a kid, my mom was usually the one to provide me comfort. But when he did speak, he chose his words wisely. I always knew what he had to say was important, and, though I may not have realized it at the time, that small speech may have been the most important thing he's ever said to me.

That first day of middle school was rough, and—I'm sorry to say—my dad's great advice was not appreciated or put to use. I would remember his words every now and then as I went through school, but it never fully resonated with me.

Fast forward to college, when I was diagnosed with anxiety and depression. I felt incredibly alone, and I would often get stuck in my own head with thoughts of self-hatred, doubt, and paralyzing

WORDS ARE INCREDIBLY POWERFUL TOOLS—AND THE WORDS THAT MAY NOT RESONATE WITH YOU TODAY MAY CHANGE YOUR LIFE THE NEXT.

fear. I became very self-focused, and it benefited no one—especially not me.

One day, amid those dark times, my dad's words came back to me. I was sitting in my dorm room when I remembered that first day of middle school. Suddenly, everything was put into perspective, and I felt moved. That was the day I decided to share my story of mental illness on social media. I shifted my focus off my pain and decided to be that "friend" to someone else who needed to hear that *they* were not alone. It turned my world around, and I have found so much more joy in my life since putting my dad's advice to use.

My dad's words aren't the only ones that have gotten me through a difficult time. In fact, since then, I have started collecting phrases and quotes from all sorts of places as part of my therapy. I've pulled quotes from Pinterest, the Bible, Instagram…even Jimmy John's lobby art (I'm not kidding—you really need to start reading their signs). I would jot the quotes down in my Notes app, or I'd write it on a Post-it and stick it on my dorm room mirror.

Words are incredibly powerful tools—and the words that may not resonate with you today may change your life the next. If you feel a connection with a phrase, I encourage you to write it down as part of your "pearls of wisdom," for you never know when it will shift your focus in the right direction.

# STEP 3

## WHAT ARE YOUR
## *PEARLS OF WISDOM?*

Throughout your life, you have most likely been given advice, read something, or watched something and then said to yourself:

> *"I love this.*
>
> *I am going to remember this forever.*
>
> *I am going to live by this."*

They may have been the kind of encouragements that inspire and awaken you to new possibilities, little "pick-me-ups" that help you believe in yourself, or supportive thoughts to turn to in times of crisis to bring hope and get you back on track.

Impactful classes, on-line courses, webinars, or workshops you've attended.

"I LOVE THIS. I AM GOING TO LIVE BY THIS. I AM GOING TO REMEMBER THIS FOREVER."

People you admire from the second exercise

Family members, friends

WHO ARE THE **GREATEST TEACHERS** *IN YOUR LIFE?*

Coaches, mentors teachers, therapists, support groups, spiritual leaders, speakers

Favorite books, podcast episodes, TedTalks, Master Classes, You Tube Videos, documentaries

**1** Think back to the great "teachers" in your life. The kind of individuals or resources that helped you understand and process the world around you, that provided guidance, motivation, and support. Who are your teachers?

Here is a list of people and resources from which you may have received such guidance.

- People you admire from Step 2 in this workbook
- Coaches, mentors, teachers, therapists, support groups
- Inspirational figures, world leaders, spiritual teachers
- Family members, friends
- Favorite books, movies, song lyrics, podcast episodes, TED Talks, master classes, YouTube videos, documentaries
- Impactful classes, online courses, webinars, workshops you've attended

MAKE A LIST OF YOUR TOP TEACHERS

_____

_____

_____

_____

_____

_____

_____

MAKE A LIST OF YOUR TOP TEACHERS (CONTINUED)

_____

_____

_____

_____

_____

_____

_____

_____

_____

_____

_____

_____

_____

_____

_____

_____

_____

_____

_____

_____

_____

_____

**2** Now, what did they say or what lesson or nugget of gold did they leave you with? Revisit your most treasured books, read your scribbles in the margins. Find your favorite notes and quotes in your phone. If you can't find the quote but know the person who said it, reach out to them. There's a great excuse to call Grandma, text your friend, or email your old sports coach. Let them know they made a difference in your life.

LIST THE MAJOR TAKEAWAYS
THAT STILL SPEAK TO YOU TODAY

_____

_____

_____

_____

_____

_____

_____

_____

_____

_____

_____

**Note:** If you can't find that many *Pearls of Wisdom* right now, do this progressively and just keep adding to your collection one Pearl at a time.

LIST THE MAJOR TAKEAWAYS
THAT STILL SPEAK TO YOU TODAY
(CONTINUED)

_____

_____

_____

_____

_____

_____

_____

_____

_____

_____

_____

_____

_____

_____

_____

_____

_____

_____

_____

_____

**3** If there are social media accounts that inspire you, revisit those, take screenshots of the posts you want to remember and add them to your Playbook.

**4** Optional: take this moment to *unfollow* accounts that don't serve you well. There are two types of follows: those that bring you energy and those that suck it away from you. Choose to unfollow the second. Look for more inspiring accounts to follow, you'll be fed more. Make those algorithms work for you.

🔖 At a certain point, the volume of "Pearls of Wisdom" you collect may become overwhelming. That's why we're excited to offer a solution for information overload with the Self!sh app. The app will allow you to organize and categorize guidance according to your needs. Whether it's tips for mental health, parenting, relationships, work, performances, fitness, sports, or anything else, you will be able to curate your own personalized Playbook for life.

# THE WHY

## EXERCISE BENEFIT

You are creating a common place to consolidate the major nuggets of gold you've acquired throughout your life, as well as any new advice and lessons you love and don't want to forget. Well, now you *won't* forget it! With your Playbook, this guidance will be in the forefront of your mind instead of hiding in the back rows of your mental library. This exercise is about making the most of the wisdom you come across, giving you a chance to revisit it again and again, and make it a part of your everyday life. And don't forget, moving forward, whenever you come across something that resonates—any guidance you want to hold on to—add it to your Playbook!

## THE SCIENCE BEHIND IT

Become a life learner! Keep adding to your Playbook. Connecting new knowledge with concepts that we already understand can significantly improve our ability to retain and recall new information. Wisdom has the power to regulate our emotions, shape our perspectives, and is closely associated with improvements in both mental and physical health. It promotes resiliency, compassion, empathy, acceptance of uncertainty, and can enhance our decision-making skills.

## PLAYBOOK ENTRY EXAMPLES
### (do what works for you!):

- Insert screenshots of your favorite Pearls of Wisdom.

- Pick inspiring pictures and write the advice and guidance you want to recall on them.

- If you are in counseling or therapy, start collecting the advice and guidance you really want to hold onto. Your Playbook will give you a tool to review it, refresh it to your memory, and increase the odds that you can integrate it into your life.

# STEP 3

## BRAIN DUMP

_____
_____
_____
_____
_____
_____
_____
_____
_____
_____
_____
_____
_____
_____
_____
_____
_____
_____
_____
_____
_____
_____
_____

# STEP 3

# SELF!SH

# STEP 3

# 4

## WHAT IS YOUR
## IMPOSSIBLE FUTURE?

" Dreams are not reality; dreams
have the power to create the
reality we are dreaming about;
all we need is the courage to
**believe in the power of dreams.** "

—*AMAR OCHANI*

*STORY BY*

## BRYAN ABRAMS

Two-time Grammy nominated singer-songwriter and
Give an Hour Ambassador

### DREAMING YOUR IMPOSSIBLE FUTURE....

This exercise reminded me of the dreaming I used to do when I was a young boy.

I learned from my great-grandmother Neely, a Choctaw Indian, that our dreams and imaginations were very powerful. And I knew that as long as I had my dreams, my imagination, and my music, I could be whoever I wanted to be, see whatever I wanted to see, and forever be free.

My father was killed when I was two years old. The only memory I have of him is when he set a puppy down on our blue 1970s shag carpet right in front of me. I got so distracted by my new furry friend that I never saw my dad leave. That would be the last time I'd ever see him. Everyone told me my dad looked exactly like Elvis Presley: tall, dark, and always well-dressed, with movie star good looks.

The father figures I would later come to know were my three stepfathers. The first was the worst. I saw him beat my mother and sister and he would have beaten me too, if he'd been able to catch me. I longed for acceptance and hoped to be adopted but my hope was never fulfilled by any of my stepfathers.

I spent a lot of time dreaming. My favorite dream was when I would fly like an eagle over unreachable places. I spent hours in front of the TV watching old Elvis Presley movies, soothing myself, pretending my father was only gone because he was on the road. I escaped through music, listening as loud as I could play it, or with headphones covering my ears to silence the noise and utter chaos happening in my life.

Music became my pulse. I'd use my imagination and see my future self grow tall and strong, slim down, and transform into this handsome musician. Music filled my lungs with air, my veins with blood, my heart with love, and my voice with song. I became the music and success was inevitable—I *knew* it.

I started a vocal group with three of my high school buddies. As the group's lead singer and songwriter, I landed a record deal with a major label and achieved several number one hit records.

We had several more in the Top Twenty, toured world stages, and recorded four studio albums.

Blessed with a golden voice, a handsome face, money, fame, and everything my younger self ever DREAMED of, I still found myself empty and broken. Nothing filled my soul. I started drinking and then using drugs. Alcohol and drugs were how I masked my fear, pushed away my sorrow, and numbed the trauma. I was an alcoholic-addict and totally lost.

On some subconscious level, for years through my struggles with addiction, mental illness, and identity issues, I must have been trying to find the eagle again in my dreams. But instead, I dreamt of a dirty, matted wolf growling at me. Addiction is a narcissistic disease. I was hurting a lot of people. I was putting my loved ones through hell. I lost their trust and I lost all confidence in myself.

Years and years later, the eagle finally returned in a dream with a message that felt grim. A message I didn't want. A message I didn't believe was possible. I will never forget the day I knew I'd had enough to drink. I prayed to my creator, as I had before, but

WHEN I WRITE SONGS, DREAMING UP AN IMPOSSIBLE FUTURE IS SORT OF WHAT I DO! I PUT MYSELF AND MY LOVED ONES IN AN AMAZING PLACE OF PEACE AND HAPPINESS!

this time, I knew I'd be freed. I knew I had to stop hiding, stop blaming, stop being selfish. I knew I had to take time to heal.

With my family's support and my newly crafted servant's heart fully beating in my chest, I am now in my fifth year of recovery. My daily management of the brain disease known as addiction is key to me keeping that wolf away knowing that the lifetime of struggles I've faced no longer define me.

I loved this exercise. It took me to a special place, a combination of what I learned from being taught about Christianity and what I learned and I'm still learning about being Choctaw Indian. It's funny because when I write songs, dreaming up an Impossible Future is sort of what I do! I put myself and my loved ones in an amazing place of peace and happiness! It is completely different than when I used to dream as a kid and picture myself with a lot of money or material things, which I thought I wanted so much.

The Impossible Future involves things that money just can't buy.... Go dream it up and who knows, you might encounter an eagle who'll guide you.

# STEP 4

## WHAT IS YOUR
## IMPOSSIBLE FUTURE?

THIS IS FUN. **You get to use your imagination and visualize your best life.**

### YOU

How do you feel?

How is your health?

What do you look like?

### PEOPLE

Who is there with you?

How do you connect with
the people in your life?

*VISUALIZE
YOUR IMPOSSIBLE*
FUTURE

### PLACE

Where do you live?

What does your home
look like?

What does the world
around you look like?

### WHAT DO YOU DO?

Do you have new talents?

What do you do
professionally?

How are your finances?

What do you do for fun?

### THE BIGGER PICTURE

Is there anything that surprises
you in this picture?

What is your contribution
to the world?

How do you feel about
your life?

**1** First, take a few beats to let go of the day, the deadlines, and the negativity, and bring your attention to this moment. Take a deep breath. And smile (research has found that a smile, even a fake-smile, releases endorphins in your brain, can give you a mood-boost, and reduce stress).

In this impossible future there are no limits. There are no obstacles. Remove all restrictions from your mind—money is not an object, there are no bills to pay, no deadlines, and you can live wherever you want. **EVERYTHING** is possible.

**2** Now, close your eyes, breathe in, and picture yourself in your dream life, ten years from now. Don't second-guess your impulses, even if it seems impossible to you in this moment. Explore all segments of your life and *be as detailed as possible*. Use your senses to see, hear, and feel. Keep asking yourself "How do I feel?" If it doesn't feel right, change it up, YOU are the creator of this story.

Sometimes, letting our imagination roam free is easier said than done. If you're finding it difficult to explore an "impossible future," try doing this exercise in your car! Yes, that's right, your car. Our cars can be peaceful capsules, away from all the hustle and bustle and obligations of our lives. Park your car in a quiet parking lot, preferably by a beautiful natural setting—a park, a secluded beach, or overlooking the golf course. Sit in silence or put on your favorite music, and give yourself permission to dream big!

Once you open your eyes, jot down everything you saw and felt. Take note of the emotions and thoughts you had and write them down. Be as detailed as possible while describing this impossible future, and try to paint a vivid picture.

# STEP 4

_____

_____

_____

_____

_____

_____

_____

_____

_____

_____

_____

_____

_____

_____

_____

_____

_____

_____

_____

_____

In this ideal future, is there anything that surprises you? What is your contribution to the world? How do you feel about your life?

_____

_____

_____

_____

_____

_____

_____

_____

_____

_____

_____

_____

_____

_____

_____

_____

_____

_____

_____

**5** Does this vision align with the values you admire in Step 2?

_____

_____

_____

_____

_____

_____

_____

_____

_____

_____

_____

_____

_____

_____

_____

_____

_____

_____

_____

_____

_____

Was everything about this vision totally impossible? Ask yourself if there are any achievable aspects in this impossible future. Circle those aspects and write down actionable steps you could take to begin working towards them.

_____

_____

_____

_____

_____

_____

_____

_____

_____

_____

_____

_____

_____

_____

_____

_____

_____

_____

# THE WHY

## EXERCISE BENEFIT

This exercise encourages you to explore your deepest desires and aspirations, open the door to new possibilities and opportunities, consider how you would feel, and reflect on how this new reality would shape your sense of fulfillment and happiness. By tapping into your imagination, and allowing yourself to DREAM, you may discover that what you thought you wanted is actually not what you truly desire.

## THE SCIENCE BEHIND IT

The Impossible Future exercise is based on the idea that we can create our own reality. By focusing on what we want and visualizing it vividly, we are more likely to achieve it. Not by magic but because new neural pathways are created that motivate us to act in accordance with our imagination. Studies have shown that creating a compelling vision of our future can have a positive impact on our emotional well-being and encourage us to achieve our goals. Dr. Ryan Niemiec, referring to this exercise as "The Best Possible Self," has noted that it can also "boost people's positive emotions, happiness levels, optimism, and hope, improve coping skills, and elevate positive expectations about the future."

PLAYBOOK ENTRY EXAMPLES
*(DO WHAT WORKS FOR YOU!):*

- Make a vision board with images that represent where your imagination took you. Take a picture of it and add it to your Playbook.

- Pair your vision with a picture that illustrates it. If there was a dog, add a dog! Add anything that will connect you to how you felt when envisioning your impossible future.

**Note**: I did this exercise back in 2006. Jay Marson, the psycho-therapist who encouraged me to do it, emphasized the idea that I should "be as detailed as possible and eliminate logistical and monetary constraints—hence impossible." I was living in New York City at the time and had no desire to move anywhere else. But my "Impossible Future" took me to "an old house, with a strong foundation—it carries our soul in its walls, in the way it is furnished…. It has objects that are meaningful to us and that we collected from places we've loved. We live outside a lot, we have a yard, with woods beyond the yard. There is an old fireplace, the fire is burning, we are on the floor, hardwood floors, there's a carpet, fluffy and white, and there is dog hair on the carpet. DOG HAIR? (WTF? I don't even like dogs)." At the time I wrote this, I loved apartment and city living (given I was going after acting roles, being in NYC seemed imperative) and thought I had no desire to move into a house (my entire childhood and into my thirties I had only lived in an urban apartment). Yet, seven years after doing this exercise, we moved out of NYC into an old house, with wetlands in the back, and lo and behold, I have become a loving dog mama. *Moral of the story: don't limit yourself based on your current situation and what you think you will need. Let your imagination run free—it will unearth your heart's deepest desires.*

# STEP 4

## BRAIN DUMP

_____

_____

_____

_____

_____

_____

_____

_____

_____

_____

_____

_____

_____

_____

_____

_____

_____

_____

_____

_____

# STEP 4

_____

_____

_____

_____

_____

_____

_____

_____

_____

_____

_____

_____

_____

_____

_____

_____

_____

_____

_____

_____

_____

_____

_____

# SELF!SH

_____

_____

_____

_____

_____

_____

_____

_____

_____

_____

_____

_____

_____

_____

_____

_____

_____

_____

_____

_____

_____

_____

_____

# STEP 4

_____

_____

_____

_____

_____

_____

_____

_____

_____

_____

_____

_____

_____

_____

_____

_____

_____

_____

_____

_____

# WHAT ARE YOUR
# DAILY WINS?

" We are all different. However
bad life may seem, there is always
something you can do, and succeed at.
**While there's life, there is hope.** "

—STEPHEN HAWKING

*STORY BY*

## ERIC CHRISTIANSEN

Acclaimed documentarian, Messenger of Hope, and
Give an Hour Ambassador

# I BELIEVE MY DAILY EXISTENCE

rests on my "spiritual fitness." Pretty darn dramatic, huh? And what does "Daily Wins" have to do with that?!? Read on. I will explain.

A poignant life lesson I've learned is that control is just an illusion. Let's get this out on the table: I am an alcoholic—a drink-until-I-die variety. I have no control once I take that first sip! But I have not had a drink in over thirty-one years. Not bragging here—it isn't me or my will-power, it is something greater than me. A power greater than myself is in control. I choose to call this power God. I need to take action in order to be "spiritually fit."

It is a tough realization to understand we are not in control of the majority of our lives. Conversely, it is still tougher to be honest with ourselves about what we *are* in control of: ourselves and our reactions to life. That is a lot of responsibility! On a daily basis, I need to look at what I can control, then I need to exercise my will over these things. I think it is best summed up by a prayer near and dear to me, the Serenity Prayer:

> *God grant me the serenity to accept the things I cannot change*
>
> *The courage to change the things I can*
>
> *And the wisdom to know the difference*

One of the many things the "Daily Wins" exercise keeps me aware of is my "side of the fence." I am in control of my willingness to get up in the morning and do the things I need to maintain my "spiritual fitness." Upon awakening, I try to consider what I can control. Gratitude is first. I can decide to be grateful. I roll out of bed and remember to thank God for another day. My first win is deciding how I am going to greet the day. It is *my decision*! Next win, I go about my routine, I walk my dogs and enjoy the air and their marvelous company. If I have the time, a twenty-minute workout. A big win for me is realizing I do have control of my time, if I do not have time in the morning, I can get up a bit earlier! Next is my daily reading (meditation), and I reflect on the reading. I then summarize and send it out to a small group of men (who are on a similar path with me) and I begin to get responses and connect. It is a win to put something out and connect with others. With this routine, I feel spiritually nourished and spiritually fit.

I so often allow myself to be controlled by unknown intangibles like time, my emotions, and even other people's thoughts and words. The big breakthrough is knowing it's all in my mind. My biggest win is realizing I have the power to decide how I am going to react! What will my action be? I used to become angry and frustrated quite often because this "unknown" was telling me the negative reaction was the go-to or I deserve that anger! So many lies. Where was that coming from? The first time I interceded with myself I realized it was my decision how I reacted! I could decide to react with compassion or love or not even react at all!!! I was free! Wow! That's a win! The "unknown" ruler of my

> **THE BIG BREAKTHROUGH IS KNOWING IT'S ALL IN MY MIND. MY BIGGEST WIN IS REALIZING I HAVE THE POWER TO DECIDE HOW I AM GOING TO REACT!**

mind has to be banished! I can decide how I react! It has to be practiced daily in order for it to become part of how I function.

This is what keeps me more than an arm's length away from the drink. The "Daily Wins" exercise puts the responsibility of how I react and what I put out to others on myself. I can take control. I am no longer a "victim" of my own emotions. I become responsible for myself. It is truly miraculous how others seem to "change" when we focus on ourselves in a healthy way. Is it others changing, or are we willing to change how we see the world? Today I am in control of my willingness. I will give myself the time to sit down and work on my "spiritual fitness." It is that fitness that will get me through this day, and today is all I have.

# STEP 5

# WHAT ARE YOUR
## DAILY WINS?

**THERE ISN'T MUCH WE *CAN* CONTROL.** We can't control the weather, the traffic, the state of the world, how things will turn out in the future, or what other people think and do.

"We cannot change the cards we are dealt, just how we play the hand," said Carnegie Mellon Professor Randy Pausch. He was battling pancreatic cancer and had just a few months to live, he ad-

YOUR DAILY WINS

❝❝

We cannot change the cards we are dealt,
just how we play the hand.
—RANDY PAUSCH

*WHAT CAN YOU CONTROL?*

ACTIONS · ATTITUDE · EFFORT

dressed his audience with a heart full of life and humor and said, "I'm dying and I'm having fun and I'm going to keep having fun every day I have left, because there's no other way to play it." He had no control over his tumors or how his body reacted to treatment, but his lecture demonstrated how he CHOSE to play his hand in the game of life.

No matter what our current circumstances may be, we can grab control of the yoke by choosing to focus on the *controllables*—our Actions, our Attitude, and our Effort.

**1** Brainstorm five to ten things you can focus on every day that are in your control. The sort of things that you know move the needle in your personal and work life. ***They help you feel better, do better, and connect better with others.*** Include any of the actionable steps you identified in your Impossible Future or The People You Admire exercises. If you get stuck, use the list on the next page.

1. _____

2. _____

3. _____

4. _____

5. _____

6. _____

7. _____

8. _____

9. _____

10. _____

# SELF!SH

**Below are a bunch of potential Daily Wins to choose from.**

**Only choose what makes sense for YOU and your specific goals!**

- Nutrition and hydration

- Fitness

- Healthy habits:

  * breathing exercises

  * journaling

  * gratitude

  * meditation

  * mindfulness

  * cold showers (known to benefit both mind and body, but I can't do it!)

- Sleep:

  * relaxing nighttime routine

  * avoiding electronics before bed

  * reading more before bed

  * keeping consistent bedtime and wake-up time

- Set up limits for:

  * technology, social media, and news intake

* sugar

* alcohol

* cigarettes

- Work habits:

  * working offline for the first hour of the day

  * tackling the three most uncomfortable things first

  * spending fifteen minutes at the end of the day to organize the next work day

  * Mono-tasking (a term coined by David E. Marlow, who states that "being able to focus on one thing completely is actually the productivity break-through we hoped would come from multitasking.")

- Relationships:

  * practice listening better

  * be more patient (perhaps with your kids!)

  * help others

  * communicate better with your partner, use "I" statements instead of "you" language

  * learn to say "I'm sorry"

  * be curious

  * stay in touch with family and friends

  * practice not gossiping or judging

  * laugh a little more, complain a little less

**CAN YOU INCLUDE ANY ACTIONABLE STEPS FROM YOUR PREVIOUS EXERCISES?**

Once you've finalized your Daily Wins, write them out in the wheel on the next page, take a photo, and print it out. Stick that wheel where you can see it throughout the day. The goal is not to get 100 percent of these but if you knock out seven out of the ten, you'll have a pretty good day. And a ten out of ten would be fan-damn-tastic!

If the word "Wins" feels too competitive and makes you wince, rename your Daily Wins with a term that speaks to you—such as your daily gains, small victories, or daily good stuff. Make up what works for you!

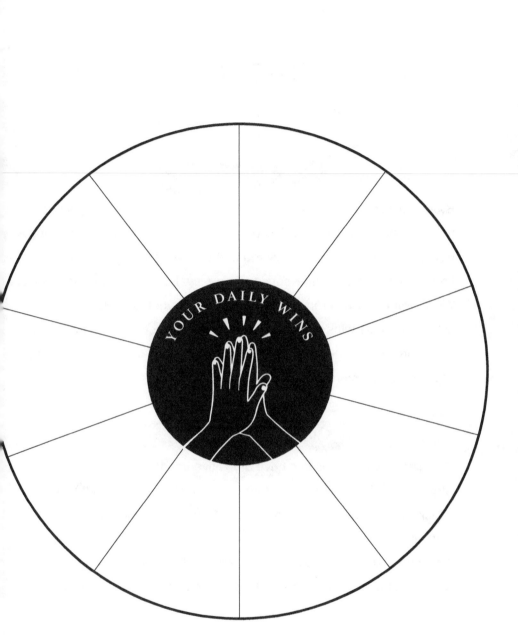

# THE WHY

## EXERCISE BENEFIT

By identifying daily habits that serve you well—and are within your control—this exercise can help bring positive momentum to your life and boost your confidence. It puts you in the driver's seat and empowers you to cultivate a greater sense of agency. Focusing on your "Daily Wins" will bring awareness and intention to your day, and regularly achieving these wins will help build that confidence even further! With each win, you'll feel more capable and in charge of your life, setting yourself up for even greater success.

## THE SCIENCE BEHIND IT

Celebrating Daily Wins can have a positive impact on our brain chemistry. Research has shown that when we achieve a goal or complete a task, the release of dopamine—the "feel good" hormone linked to motivation—can reinforce the behavior and motivate us to repeat it in the future. Attaching positive reinforcement to supportive behaviors can lead to a positive feedback loop of motivation and success.

PLAYBOOK ENTRY EXAMPLES
(DO WHAT WORKS FOR YOU!):

- Add your Daily Wins in your Playbook and stick them on a board in your home or office to be reminded throughout the day!

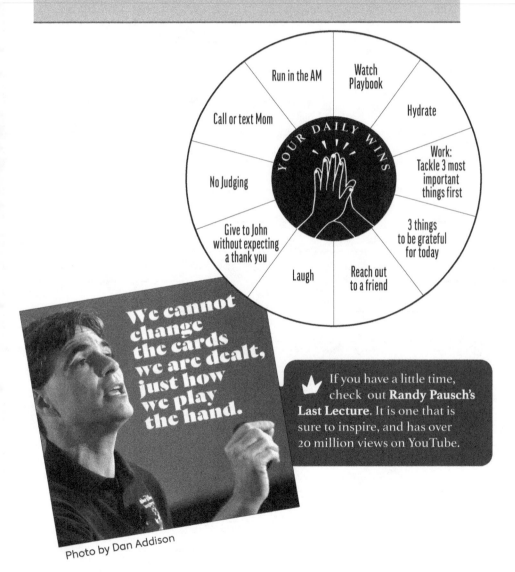

YOUR DAILY WINS

Run in the AM

Watch Playbook

Hydrate

Work: Tackle 3 most important things first

3 things to be grateful for today

Reach out to a friend

Laugh

Give to John without expecting a thank you

No Judging

Call or text Mom

We cannot change the cards we are dealt, just how we play the hand.

Photo by Dan Addison

If you have a little time, check out **Randy Pausch's Last Lecture**. It is one that is sure to inspire, and has over 20 million views on YouTube.

# STEP 5

## BRAIN DUMP

_____

_____

_____

_____

_____

_____

_____

_____

_____

_____

_____

_____

_____

_____

_____

_____

_____

_____

_____

_____

_____

_____

## STEP 5

_____

_____

_____

_____

_____

_____

_____

_____

_____

_____

_____

_____

_____

_____

_____

_____

_____

_____

_____

_____

_____

_____

_____

# SELF!SH

---
---
---
---
---
---
---
---
---
---
---
---
---
---
---
---
---
---
---
---
---
---
---
---
---
---

# STEP 5

_____

_____

_____

_____

_____

_____

_____

_____

_____

_____

_____

_____

_____

_____

_____

_____

_____

_____

_____

_____

# WHAT ARE YOUR NARRATIVES?

> "Your thoughts are like people that knock on the front door of your house. You can't control who walks up and knocks. **You can control which ones you let in and entertain as guests.**"
>
> —BOB ROTELLA

*STORY BY*

## STEPHANIE SZOSTAK

Actor, author of this workbook, and Give an Hour Ambassador

## I'M GENERALLY PRETTY HAPPY,

I smile a lot, but inside I sometimes crumble into pieces. My Achilles' heel for a number of years has been feeling stupid, really stupid, like a dumbass. Put me in a situation where I feel like I don't fit in, like I'm an outsider, like I'm the only one in the group who doesn't know something, and I will sink under a deluge of negative self-talk and self-flagellation. In an instant, my confidence can poof—evaporate and be replaced with feelings of inadequacy, shame, and isolation. These feelings permeate my earliest memories. Traveling to the United States to visit my dad's family, I remember my parents dropping me off to play with other kids and I'd ask my dad again and again, "You told them, right? You told them I don't speak English? Make sure you tell them. Otherwise, they're going to think I'm stupid." Five years old and that's when this pattern started for me. By now, it's pretty automatic.

This summer, I was at a birthday party with my husband in our small town in Connecticut. These were new friends and we didn't know that many people there. I was introduced to this guy whose name I thought was Gary. Gary looked pretty cool, he didn't have the suburban golf uniform most men wear in my neck of the woods (and I'm not saying there's anything wrong with golf shirts, my husband rocks a good golf shirt), but this man had his own style, and it wasn't for show either, he just looked, for lack of a better word, coooool. So I'm talking to him, and it turns out he's a musician—an artist, yep, I knew it.

His name is Harry not Gary. And Harry just came back from Barcelona where he was performing. Wow. I dive in deeper; I ask where he's from, what led him to Connecticut. He got a music deal at eighteen years old that brought him from New Orleans to NYC. Amazing. I have to say I was pretty impressed and most of all because Harry was so humble and kind. How refreshing.

The night went on, I babbled with all the fabulous guests, the cake came out, candles were blown, and home we went. As we drove away, my husband turned to me, seeming slightly amused and said, "You know who that was, right?" Uh-oh. No, I didn't, and in that moment, I knew I should have. Gary who was Harry was none other than Harry Connick Jr. Holy sh*t. Wow. What a nice guy, and *oops, I did it again!* I'm such an idiot! Now I wish this was one isolated incident but unfortunately this sort of thing happens to me all the time. The thing where everyone knows something except me. And it makes me shrink. I feel like a royal idiot, the king's fool here to amuse everyone. I am over fifty years old, come on! Get a grip! Who gives a f*ck? I still do.

But less than I used to! After all, I'm able to tell you all about it in a book.

The single most helpful SKILL I learned for this type of situation was from Coach Pete Carroll and high-performance psychologist, Michael Gervais. They teach an online course all about mindset called "Finding Your Best," and they have a whole section on self-talk and epic thoughts. What the heck is an epic thought, I remember thinking. I had no clue but I wanted one. Dr. Gervais explains that confidence (and I'm paraphrasing here)

AN EPIC THOUGHT IS A GOOD THOUGHT OR A POSITIVE GO-TO PHRASE CRAFTED BY YOU AND HERE'S THE KEY: YOU HAVE TO BELIEVE IT.

comes from *what you say to yourself about yourself.* In other words, our skills, our past achievements, our preparation can all help feed our confidence, but if our self-talk turns to trash, our confidence can evaporate in an instant. And here is what Dr. Gervais recommends: create epic thoughts for yourself. An epic thought is a good thought or a positive go-to phrase crafted by you and here's the key: you have to believe it. It can't be just some random positive affirmation that you half-believe. It's got to be anchored in truth, with legit evidence from your life that confirms this statement is valid to you. No one needs to hear that thought, no one needs to believe it, just YOU.

So what's my epic thought? "I come from a different culture; I think differently. I bring value to this team." You may think it's hokey, corny, laughable...and that's okay. It's *my* epic thought. I believe it and have examples to support it. Now, you go and create your own epic thoughts!

# STEP 6

# WHAT ARE YOUR
# NARRATIVES?

**THIS IS ABOUT OUR SELF-TALK, THE VOICE IN OUR HEADS (AND WE ALL HAVE ONE).**

Our narratives are the stories we regularly tell ourselves. They are repeated and confirmed in our heads again and again, often without us even realizing it. They are shaped by our past experiences and impact how we see the world and experience life.

I have one friend who continually says, *"I have the best parking karma,"* and when I am with him, well, we do find great spots. I have another friend who says, "I have such bad luck with cars," and the poor thing continues to have cars break down on her.

*Are the stories we tell ourselves true?* **Can our inner dialogue turn into a self-fulfilling prophecy?**

In his book *Chatter*, psychologist and neuroscientist Ethan Kross explains that **our inner voice is highly impactful**, not only **on our thoughts and feelings**, but **it also can influence and color everything around us**. Depending on what we say to ourselves, we basically have the power to change **how we see the world and "damage all that we hold dear—our health, our hopes, and our relationships."**

**BRAINSTORM**

**1** What are some of the usual triggers in your life that make you irritated, annoyed, or angry? DUMP it all below!

_____

_____

_____

_____

_____

_____

_____

_____

_____

_____

_____

_____

_____

_____

_____

_____

_____

_____

What people do you spend time with that tend to throw you off your game, causing you to feel insecure, anxious, frustrated, irritable, or envious?

_____

_____

_____

_____

_____

_____

_____

_____

 What places or social situations do the same? What are those moments for you? Write them down.

_____

_____

_____

_____

_____

_____

_____

_____

Now think about the inner-dialogue you typically have in these situations. What does your self-talk sound like? Write it down.

---

_____

_____

_____

_____

_____

_____

_____

_____

_____

_____

_____

_____

_____

_____

_____

_____

_____

_____

_____

How is that voice in your head sounding? Is it kind, compassionate, and supportive? Or does it chip away at your confidence and hold you back? Does it repeat on a loop and become all-consuming? Does it dwell on things that are beyond your control?

_____

_____

_____

_____

_____

_____

_____

_____

_____

In *The Feeling Good Handbook*, Dr. David D. Burns points out that "although these negative thoughts are often distorted and illogical, they can seem deceptively realistic, so you believe things really are as bad as you think they are."

We all do this; we all get caught in "thinking traps" or cognitive distortions.

The (very) good news is that YOU can be the writer and the director in this story. You have the power to rewrite these narratives! Create better ones. Those reruns are getting old. Tell some new stories that serve you well.

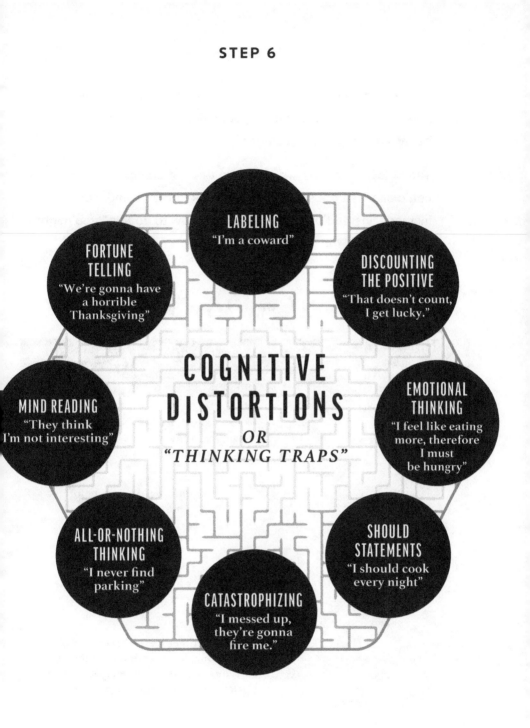

**6** Go back to bullet number four, and one by one, on the next page, create new versions of your self-talk. The examples below can help you get started.

The below examples are written in the first person, but you could also use the second person or your own name. For instance, instead of "I got this, I know how to do this," you might prefer to say "You got this John, you know how to do this."

## CREATE NEW NARRATIVES

| From "*this*" | To "*THIS*" |
|---|---|
| "This is going to suck." | "I actually don't know how it's going to go. I'm going to focus on (pick three constructive things in your control)." |
| "I can't do this. It's too much." | "I've done hard things before. One step at a time. Focus on the process." |
| "I'll never get the job." | "I don't know if I'll get the job. What does it mean for me to do the best I can in this scenerio?" |
| "They are always ignoring me and trying to put me down." | "It sometimes feels like they aren't listening, but I remind myself that everyone has their own perspectives and priorities. I will continue offering my suggestions with an open mind." |
| "I'm an idiot." | "I'm learning, I'm allowed to make mistakes. I am growing." |

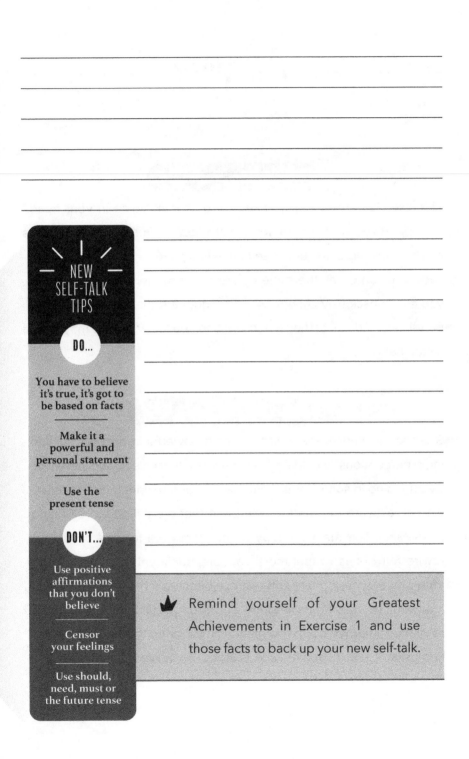

**NEW SELF-TALK TIPS**

**DO...**

You have to believe it's true, it's got to be based on facts

Make it a powerful and personal statement

Use the present tense

**DON'T...**

Use positive affirmations that you don't believe

Censor your feelings

Use should, need, must or the future tense

Remind yourself of your Greatest Achievements in Exercise 1 and use those facts to back up your new self-talk.

# THE WHY

## EXERCISE BENEFIT

This exercise will help you take notice of that "voice in your head." Unsupportive narratives you form over a lifetime from past experiences can become ingrained and lead to habitual patterns of behaviors. However, you can break the cycle by creating new self-talk. By doing so, you can consciously change your thought patterns, boost your mood, better respond to situations, and what do you know...things may unfold a little better.

## THE SCIENCE BEHIND IT

Science has shown that self-talk has a powerful impact on our feelings, perceptions (including how we view ourselves), and behaviors. By engaging in some "brain remodeling," and rewriting our narratives, we can activate the parts of the brain that are linked to self-related processing. This means that by changing our self-talk, we can literally rewire our brains to feel more capable, confident, and empowered. With practice, supportive self-talk can become a habit that uplifts and motivates us, helping us respond to challenges with greater ease and resilience, improve our performance (in life or on the set!), and overall find greater satisfaction in various areas of our lives.

## PLAYBOOK ENTRY EXAMPLES (DO WHAT WORKS FOR YOU!):

- Create one or more visuals with your new "self-talk"

- List your Epic thoughts

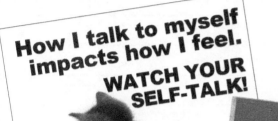

How I talk to myself impacts how I feel. **WATCH YOUR SELF-TALK!**

**SELF-TALK**

| ⊗ INSTEAD OF | ⊘ TRY THIS |
|---|---|
| SHAMING YOURSELF | ASK FOR HELP |
| COMPARING YOURSELF | GET BACK TO YOUR WHY |
| PUSHING YOURSELF | TAKE TIME OFF |
| OVERTHINKING | LISTEN TO MUSIC |
| CRITICAL SELF TALK | CELEBRATE SMALL WINS |

| From "this" | To "THIS" |
|---|---|
| "This is going to suck." | "I actually don't know how it's going to go. I'm going to focus on (pick three constructive things in your control)." |
| "I can't do this. It's too much." | "I've done hard things before. One step at a time. Focus on the process." |
| "I'll never get the job." | "I don't know if I'll get the job. What does it mean for me to do the best I can in this scenerio?" |
| "They are always ignoring me and trying to put me down." | "It sometimes feels like they aren't listening, but I remind myself that everyone has their own perspectives and priorities. I will continue offering my suggestions with an open mind." |
| "I'm an idiot." | "I'm learning, I'm allowed to make mistakes. I am growing." |

# STEP 6

## BRAIN DUMP

# STEP 6

_____

_____

_____

_____

_____

_____

_____

_____

_____

_____

_____

_____

_____

_____

_____

_____

_____

_____

_____

_____

_____

_____

_____

# SELF!SH

_____

_____

_____

_____

_____

_____

_____

_____

_____

_____

_____

_____

_____

_____

_____

_____

_____

_____

_____

_____

_____

_____

_____

# STEP 6

_____

_____

_____

_____

_____

_____

_____

_____

_____

_____

_____

_____

_____

_____

_____

_____

_____

_____

_____

_____

# HOW DO YOU
# FIND AND
# SPREAD JOY?

> " Enjoy the little things in life for
> one day you'll look back and realize
> **they were the big things.** "
>
> —*KURT VONNEGUT*

## STORY BY

### NICKIE SILVERSTEIN

Veteran and Give an Hour Consultant

## IT'S THE MOST WONDERFUL TIME OF THE YEAR.

That is what I truly believe about the forty or so days between November fifteenth and January first. And it all goes back to my formative years as a child. But as I sit and wonder why joy over-comes me when I think about this special time of year, it comes down to one reason...family.

My memories are full of music, food, laughing, snow, shiny lights, sur-prise, games, and puzzles, and in the center of all the memories is family. As a young child, both sets of my grandparents lived close. What that meant was family gatherings with aunts, uncles, cousins, and people that were "like family."

My parents and grandparents set the stage for feeling warmth, joy, wonder, love, and magic. As I got older, and now as a parent myself, I learned this time of year can be hectic, busy, and even stressful. And I know that getting together with family can also present stress. But when I was a young child, the adults in my life never put that burden on me or complained about how much they had to do to make the holiday season absolutely magical!

Every Christmas, after the gifts were opened and the big meal was served and consumed, in an eighth of the time it took to make, my cousin, brother, and I put on our own show that we spent the whole afternoon choreographing (I use that word loosely). We would go around my grandparents' house selling tickets to our show. And whether they wanted to or not, everyone bought a ticket, sat down, and with their full attention watched us then applauded like we just danced the "Waltz of the Flowers" from *The Nutcracker*.

It is with great joy that I am now on the receiving end of that tradition and get to watch my children when they say, "Watch me, mom. Come watch the dance I put together." The holidays are a bit different for my kiddos than they were for me. We do not live near family, but we have wonderful people in our community and friends that feel like family. And while we have added a few commercialized traditions to our holiday season (dare I say Elf on the Shelf), we are sure to keep the ones that mattered the most to my family as a child. Maybe someday my great-great grandchild will wake up on Christmas morning and before they touch their stocking or presents, they will sit and listen to their dad read *The Birth of Jesus.*

Reflecting on these memories and the feelings they give me allows me to realize that I can and do incorporate some of these special things into my daily life. I just need to stop and pay attention to them with new intention. For example, while it is not Christmas Eve dinner, my kids love Taco Tuesday or Pizza Friday. By recognizing that those nights are just as special to my family, it allows me to enjoy them with a renewed spirit. Recently our family started sharing Taco Tuesday with two families in our neighborhood that are going through some medical situations and could use a little help. When my kids deliver the meals, they are involved in showing care and sharing joy with others. I am confident that this little act of kindness is teaching them that giving can be just as joyful as receiving.

> I CAN AND DO INCORPORATE SOME OF THESE SPECIAL THINGS INTO MY DAILY LIFE. I JUST NEED TO STOP AND PAY ATTENTION TO THEM WITH NEW INTENTION.

## STEP 7

# HOW DO YOU
# FIND AND SPREAD JOY?

### PURE
### AND SIMPLE
### JOY

*watching the sun rise when I wake up early enough*

**making people laugh • watching funny movies**

*precious moments of solitude • a meaningful smile with a stranger*

**bringing people together • checking in with a loved one**

*working out • singing in the shower*

**hiking though the woods with my dog**

*tennis • cooking • dancing • running*

**driving with loud music and windows down**

*helping someone without expecting a thank you*

**eating ice cream out of a cone**

*my kids' laughter*

**1** What brings YOU joy? Is joy something we can control? Can we go looking for it? Can we create an atmosphere of JOY for ourselves? For others?

Think back to joyful memories in your life. Where were you? Who were you with? What were you doing?

_____

_____

_____

_____

_____

_____

_____

_____

_____

_____

_____

_____

_____

_____

_____

_____

Who are the people in your life who bring you joy and light you up? And what specifically do you love doing with them?

_____

_____

_____

_____

_____

_____

_____

_____

_____

_____

_____

_____

_____

_____

_____

_____

_____

_____

**3** What are the activities in your life that do the same?

_____

_____

_____

_____

_____

_____

_____

_____

_____

_____

_____

_____

_____

_____

_____

_____

_____

_____

_____

_____

What simple pleasures of life bring you joy? Does nature bring you joy? If so, what about it do you love? Is it a certain smell, a certain sound?

_____

_____

_____

_____

_____

_____

_____

_____

_____

_____

_____

_____

_____

_____

_____

_____

_____

_____

_____

How do you spread joy? How have you done so in the past? (Other than giving thanks in November and gifts in December.) To your loved ones? To people in your community? To strangers you encounter?

_____

_____

_____

_____

_____

_____

_____

_____

 Is there room in your life to receive and give more joy? If yes, how?

_____

_____

_____

_____

_____

_____

_____

_____

Now that you've recognized the joy in your life, take a moment to practice a little gratitude. Observe the gifts that improve the quality of your life. Is it having the ability to go for a walk, a healthy body, a supportive partner, a job that pays the bills, the opportunity to learn a new skill?

# THE WHY

## EXERCISE BENEFIT

This exercise is all about the simplicity of joy and the space in your heart you can create for it. It will help you recognize that even hard days can be softened with a little joy and gratitude if we remember to make space for it. Your Playbook entries and the images of people and activities that bring you joy will remind you to intentionally prioritize, seek and spread JOY.

## THE SCIENCE BEHIND IT

Joy is exciting! Experiencing positive emotions, such as joy can increase creativity, problem-solving abilities, and overall well-being, including our resilience to stress. In addition, spreading joy through acts of kindness, and practicing gratitude can release neurotransmitters like dopamine, serotonin, and oxytocin, leading to immediate mood enhancement and long-term health benefits such as lower blood pressure, improved heart-health, self-esteem and optimism. So go ahead, spread some joy today—not only will you get an instant mood boost, you'll also make a positive impact in the world!

## PLAYBOOK ENTRY EXAMPLES
### *(DO WHAT WORKS FOR YOU!):*

- All the answers from questions one to six can go in your Playbook. Choose meaningful visuals to pair them with—pictures of your family and friends, nature, sports, art, your happy places!

- A reminder to "Practice Gratitude" and "Savor and Give Joy" could also be added to your Daily Wins.

# STEP 7

## BRAIN DUMP

_____
_____
_____
_____
_____
_____
_____
_____
_____
_____
_____
_____
_____
_____
_____
_____
_____
_____
_____
_____
_____
_____

# STEP 7

# SELF!SH

_____

_____

_____

_____

_____

_____

_____

_____

_____

_____

_____

_____

_____

_____

_____

_____

_____

_____

_____

_____

_____

_____

_____

# STEP 7

STEP

*8*

## WHAT IS YOUR
## LIFE PHILOSOPHY?

" My mission in life is **not merely to
survive, but to thrive;** and to do so
with some passion, some compassion,
some humor, and some style. "

—*MAYA ANGELOU*

STORY BY

## ALLEN LEVI SIMMONS

Author, motivational speaker, podcast host, and Give
an Hour Ambassador

---

## "BOMBS OVER BAGHDAD, BOOM! BOMBS OVER AFGHANISTAN, BOOM!

*How did I get into this?
Death, death is every-
where! Mirror Mirror on
the wall, who am I after
twin towers fall? I am no
longer disguised with
camouflage desert gear;
I am clicking my heels
at attention praying
for God to get me out
of here! These combat
scars mark my soul;
bullet rounds were
shot to part my body from my soul.*

*I just can't recognize who I am. My God, I can't even rec-
ognize whose I am! Who am I? These wars have us asking
questions like, who am I, what am I, why am I here? I stand
here mesmerized that my body didn't comply when that
RPG landed a few feet next to me. My body went some-
where in the air or maybe the blast pushed me against
the surface of the earth; I am not sure. I am not sure how
I got to this place where my ears are ringing like a smoke
detector, my heartbeat singing loudly, slowly fading into
a whisper. I didn't come home the same! I couldn't gather
the pieces of my brain, the thesis to my pain. How could we
come home the same?*

*Gun in my hand, pills on my bed, Bible on my nightstand.
Paranoia tiptoeing through the hallway of my home. Gun
in my mouth and my finger on the trigger; I was knocking
on the doors of heaven wondering if anyone was home?*

*Thoughts scrambling in my head, panic attack as I
contemplated blowing a hole through my head! I felt
like someone was waiting under my bed! I wanted to die
quickly before I laid down for the last time, to finally rest
my head.*

*My home was no longer a home, it was my new war zone.
Every time I opened the door to my home, I had my pistol
ready. Every time I checked the closet, I held my pistol
steady. Every time I looked behind the shower curtains, my
mind was always ready. Why? There was no one chasing
me, there was no one in there, it was just me and me. I*

*didn't even know myself and the whole time I was fighting wars, I was fighting against me.*

*From sea to shiny sea I've lost pieces of my soul because I had forgotten about me. I forgot the power of prayer! I forgot that my God was there! I had forgotten that He has always cared for me. I was born again, I found my way within. I had to distance myself from me. The war veteran with traumatic brain injury and PTSD."*

—Excerpt from Allen Levi Simmons' book of poetry *Can I Speak?*

My name is Allen Levi Simmons, and I am a survivor.

My life philosophy is, Never Stop, Never Quit, Repeat!™

After war, I wasn't sure if I would ever have a "normal life." I struggled financially, mentally, and emotionally for over four years. I found myself at a crossroads. I was back in college at the age of twenty-six and I was on academic probation because my GPA had dropped to a 2.0. While on the campus of UNC Charlotte, I felt defeated and my life flashed before my eyes. Everything I went

> ONCE I FELT THAT MY SOUL HAD AGREED WITH MY HEART AND MIND, THESE WORDS FORMULATED WITHIN, "NEVER STOP, NEVER QUIT, REPEAT!"

through during war and afterwards came whisking through my memories. Every failed attempt at college screamed at me from the hallways of my mind. "I am tired of giving up. I am tired of failing. I am tired of feeling inadequate. I am tired...."

It was on this day that I decided that I would not give up, I would not fold, and that I would rise above my own expectations for myself. Once I felt that my soul had agreed with my heart and mind, these words formulated within, "Never Stop, Never Quit, Repeat!"

REPEAT UNTIL YOU GET WHAT YOU WANT OUT OF LIFE AND YOUR EXPERIENCES!

You deserve to see yourself rise above the trauma, the failure, and the pain of your past. You deserve to have a philosophy that will take you over the hills of doubt, fear, and anxiety. Make your life philosophy one you believe in and make it speak to your soul.

# STEP 8

# WHAT IS YOUR
# LIFE PHILOSOPHY?

**DO YOU EVER FEEL LIKE YOU'RE SET ON THE WRONG FREQUENCY?** Dialed in on the AM with too much interference and too much noise? At odds with yourself? Your Life Philosophy is about making YOU feel in tune with who you are.

Finding your Life Philosophy can take a bit of time. Be patient with this one! **All the work you've done in the previous exercises can help you craft your Life Philosophy.**

Now what the heck is it? It's a key phrase that guides and points you back to your North Star. Performance Psychologist, Michael Gervais refers to it as a Personal Philosophy. It is your mission statement. Your motto. Your mantra. It is whatever YOU want to call it.

**Your Life Philosophy captures the essence of who you are, your values, and core beliefs. It is a barometer for what truly matters to you.**

You don't *need* one, but why not have one for when the going gets tough—because it will. When it does get tough, you can whisper this to yourself and perhaps find your way through a challenge by bringing your focus back to your guiding principles, and aspirations.

**Your Life Philosophy isn't supposed to sound fancy, cool, or good to anyone but YOU.** It is meant to encourage you to bring YOURSELF to life, frankly and unapologetically.

A famous acting teacher named Uta Hagen said, *"Instead of losing yourself in the part, bring yourself to the part."* We may not all be actors, but we all are players in life, and at times we get lost and worn down. We may find ourselves overwhelmed by the challenges we face, doubt our capacity to make sound decisions, get caught up in other people's opinions, and lose sight of how to fully embrace and engage with life.

*Your Life Philosophy empowers you to bring yourself fully to the part of life, to where your magic, authenticity, and purpose lie.*

## YOUR LIFE PHILOSOPHY

It captures the
**ESSENCE OF WHO YOU ARE,** your **VALUES** and **CORE BELIEFS.**
It is a barometer for
**WHAT TRULY MATTERS TO YOU.**

What you can focus on when everything else seems to be falling apart.

How you strive to connect with yourself, with others and with life.

What empowers you to bring yourself fully to where your magic, authenticity and purpose lie.

# SELF!SH

**1** Look back through all the previous exercises:

Everything that inspires, motivates, and helps you navigate challenges. Identify the key words and phrases that best capture who you are and what you stand for, and write them down below.

**KEY WORDS AND PHRASES THAT RESONATE WITH ME**

_____

_____

_____

_____

_____

_____

_____

_____

_____

_____

_____

_____

_____

_____

_____

_____

_____

Complete the following statement: "This is how I want to show up in life for myself and others…"

Write away. Get the words out. Don't limit yourself. Write as many words as you want. It's real—it's unique—it's you.

**FREE WRITING**

_____

_____

_____

_____

_____

_____

_____

_____

_____

_____

_____

_____

_____

_____

_____

_____

_____

## FREE WRITING (CONTINUED)

**3** Try shortening what you have to just a paragraph. Cross out what's redundant. Underline what resonates.

MAKE IT SHORTER

_____

_____

_____

_____

_____

_____

_____

_____

**4** Continue the process, chip away, and try to eliminate some more until you have one sentence or phrase.

EVEN SHORTER

_____

_____

_____

_____

_____

_____

**5** Read it OUT LOUD. Ask yourself:

- How did that sound?
- Does this ring true to who I am?
- How did it feel to say that?
- Does this encourage me?
- Would that phrase be a good guide in making decisions?

Let's say you were thinking of buying a new car and you're hesitating between two: a bold, flashy car that you love and a more practical, sensible car that might be a better fit for your lifestyle. Would quietly saying your life philosophy to yourself help guide you in making the decision? If your life philosophy emphasizes pursuing your passions and taking risks, you may lean towards the bold car. But if it emphasizes family, humility, and financial stability, you might opt for the more sensible car. Whether you're buying a car, changing careers, pursuing a creative endeavor, or even asking someone on a date, your life philosophy can serve as valuable guide in making decisions, and pursuing opportunities that align with your values, aspirations and vision for a fulfilling life.

**Keep in mind that finding your Life Philosophy can take a bit of time.** Live with it for a while. Test it out, see if it centers you when you say it or read it. If not, tweak it, change it, go back to your brainstorm. It should be an expression of who you are and who you strive to be.

# THE WHY

Creating your Life Philosophy is an incredible opportunity to reflect on your journey so far. Through the previous exercises, you get to take a conscious look back at your accomplishments, values, and aspirations, as well as the lessons you've learned along the way. By doing this, you can identify the common threads that have guided you through life and use them to create a unique and powerful philosophy that will serve as your guide, calling you to action, and setting a benchmark for decision-making. This is your chance to put words to the principles that drive you and craft a philosophy that will inspire you to live your best life.

## THE SCIENCE BEHIND IT

A Life Philosophy that is meaningful and uplifting can be a powerful guide for personal growth and motivation. According to Dr. Michael Gervais, it can assist us in living in harmony with our true selves. By regularly repeating our Philosophy to ourselves, we can approach life with clear intention, increase our drive, gain a sense of purpose, and prevent intrusive unsupportive thoughts from taking over.

PLAYBOOK ENTRY EXAMPLES
*(DO WHAT WORKS FOR YOU!):*

- Write your Life Philosophy over an inspiring background or personal picture. Get in the habit of saying it in your head. Practice saying it out loud every day.

- If you journal, write it down every day.

Be Curious.
Keep on
Exploring.

"
Start where you are.
Use what you have.
Do what you can.
—
ARTHUR ASHE

I dare to
go after my
truth,
with love and
humor

Be the change
you wish to see
in the world.
—
Mahatma Gandhi

# STEP 8

## BRAIN DUMP

_____
_____
_____
_____
_____
_____
_____
_____
_____
_____
_____
_____
_____
_____
_____
_____
_____
_____
_____
_____

# SELF!SH

---
---
---
---
---
---
---
---
---
---
---
---
---
---
---
---
---
---
---
---
---
---
---
---
---

# STEP 8

# NEXT STEPS

## CONGRATULATIONS!

You dug in, you took some time for yourself, and you explored your personal lived experience. You have a clearer idea of who you are, including:

- The strengths and characteristics you bring to the world
- The values and principles you aspire to live by
- The hopes and dreams that make you come alive
- The building blocks that bring you inner strength, clarity, peace, and joy

You have a better understanding of the kind of life you want to live.

In 1967, Martin Luther King Jr. asked a group of students at Barratt Junior High in Philadelphia, "What is in your life's blueprint? You're in the process of building the structure of your lives. And the question is whether you have a proper, solid, and sound blueprint."

Now, you're probably way past junior high, but are we ever done building the structure of our lives? Your Playbook is that *blueprint*. It is your foundation.

**The challenge now is figuring out how you give staying power to all the work you've done.**

How do you cultivate the empowering strategies you've identified and create a ripple effect that elevates the quality of your life?

One last story...

I started this book by telling you my dad was one of my most inspirational teachers in golf and in life. What I didn't tell you is that for all of the fine qualities the man possesses, he is oftentimes completely unpleasant to play golf with. Golf is his passion and it is his life. How his golf game is going, his mood will follow. If he hits a bad shot, he explodes like a volcano. It can come out of nowhere and can wreck the atmosphere of a game. He can also wreck a tee box, a sand trap, or his own golf clubs. Sometimes I'll get to a green and look back and see him a hundred yards back in the fairway repairing the turf he just tore up with his wedge.

On a recent summer visit, my dad and I were scheduled to play in a tournament after my husband had told me "Your turn. You're playing with him. Have fun." On the morning of, my inner dialogue was something like this "I don't want to do this, why did I agree to do this? I can't stand watching an eighty-seven-year-old act like a four-year-old, it is so embarrassing. Who are we going to play with? What are they going to think? Should I warn them on the first tee?"

Then I started in on myself, "Why am I so mean? He is old, I should be happy to have the opportunity to play with him. He's gotten so much better; he makes an effort. What a horrible daughter I am."

This conversation was pretty much going in a loop in my head for fifteen minutes. I made myself miserable. And **I was going to be the unpleasant one to be with.**

So I went downstairs, got my coffee, came back upstairs alone, and hit PLAY on my Playbook. I needed a mind shift. All my strategies for managing potentially difficult situations came back to me, feeding the gratitude of my mind rather than the dread. After just a few minutes, I had a gentle nudge in the direction of Love and Acceptance. I reconnected with the better part of myself: compassion and some much needed HUMOR. Suddenly, I was looking forward to marveling at the art of his club toss. I would potentially even get to watch the reaction of our playing partners as they would attempt to translate his English curse words to French. We didn't win the tournament that day, but we had a wonderful father-daughter day on the course and there wasn't a single outburst from my dad. Ultimately, my experience probably changed due to the energy I ended up bringing to the first tee box that day. By the way, I didn't end up warning our playing partners; heck, they were our competitors and my father's antics can be a competitive weapon.

Your Playbook won't magically make life's challenges disappear, but it may just help you turn your "father's club toss" into a golden opportunity to level up your mental game! With daily mental fitness practice, you'll learn to **shift your focus to what truly benefits you and those around you. Our minds can be tricky beasts, but with practice, we can learn to harness the power of attention and intention.** So why not give it a shot and see what beautiful things can happen when you start focusing on what serves you well?

> **TRUE PROGRESS TAKES TIME. IT'S NOT A ONE-TIME EFFORT, IT'S A DAILY COMMITMENT.**

**To be continued...by you.**

**① PRACTICE YOUR MENTAL FITNESS EVERY DAY.**

My father-in-law is a retired Air Force Colonel and Command Pilot with over seven thousand accident-free flying hours in more than twenty different airplanes, including two combat years in Vietnam. When I asked him about his greatest accomplishment, he said, "Arriving from point A to B safely for thirty years," and that a critical part of this success was the discipline required for mission planning and the use of a checklist (a Playbook)! Imagine if you had your own checklist before you take off for the day! Take a few minutes to go through your personalized checklist— your Playbook, and make it a part of your daily mental prep. If you choose to take this new approach, your odds of daily success will increase significantly (his words, not mine).

Introducing a new habit into our lives can be challenging—who needs another thing to do?! James Clear, the author of **Atomic Habits,** suggests pairing new habits with existing ones. He calls it "habit stacking." So, to introduce a new habit, you simply add it onto one you already do every day.

- Do you drink coffee every morning? Watch your Playbook while sipping on your cup of java.

- Do you spend time in the water-closet? Watch your Playbook during your morning constitutional.

- Do you meditate or exercise? Watch your Playbook, right after or right before.

**②** **WHEN YOU NEED A MIND SHIFT** before a big event or when you feel just plain stuck, crack open your Playbook and let it give your heart, mind, and soul the boost they need. Take a few minutes to do a 180 on your frame of mind.

**③** **KEEP YOUR PLAYBOOK UP TO DATE.** When you come across something that speaks to you, add it to your Playbook—whether it's a piece of advice you don't want to forget, a recent milestone you're proud of, notes from your therapy sessions, or a new goal you're setting for yourself. Everything that matters to you gets a spot in your Playbook! **Your Playbook will evolve and change with you as you continue to learn, grow, and transform.**

**Your feedback matters!** If the Self!sh workbook has brought you joy, and if your Playbook is making a positive impact in your life, we'd love to hear from you. Send us an email or share a short video with us at myplaybook@selfishplaybook.com.

### WITH MUCH GRATITUDE, WE HOPE YOUR PLAYBOOK WILL EMPOWER YOU ON A LIFELONG JOURNEY OF DISCOVERY, LEARNING, AND PROGRESS.

# GIVE AN HOUR CONTRIBUTORS LONG BIOS

**BRYAN ABRAMS** is a two-time Grammy-nominated, American Music Award winner, two-time Soul Train Award-winning R&B/pop singer-songwriter, and an Oklahoma Music Hall of Fame inductee. Bryan was the original lead singer, front man, and founding member of Color Me Badd. Having faced many public challenges, including substance use disorders, a life-long battle with obesity, and tensions within the group he founded, Abrams is painfully aware of the toll that being self-sacrificing can take on a person's mental health. Abrams found himself at rock bottom due to his addictions and was inspired to take his power back only by the desperation and disappointment he witnessed in the eyes of his wife and daughters. Having lived with addiction for over twenty-five years, Abrams has now put his focus on his mental and physical health and is proudly multiple years into his recovery. Abrams' zest for music has returned and prompted him to dive into the vault of songs written and set aside over the decades. Bryan wants people to know they are not alone.

**ERIC CHRISTIANSEN** is an acclaimed documentarian who has built his life's work around socially responsible filmmaking that educates, inspires, and most importantly heals. Christiansen, a seven-time Southwestern Region Emmy Award recipient, explores the impact of trauma, how we adapt to grief, the resilience of the human spirit, and how a powerful platform for hope can help trauma survivors begin the vigilant journey of healing. All of his films have been transformative in the recovery process for thousands of people whose lives have been compromised mentally, spiritually, and physically by trauma. Leveraged as educational tools by top mental health institutions, Eric's films migrate from the entertainment arena into environments that help additional audiences navigate the profound collateral damage trauma creates not only on the individual, but the family and community as well. Eric's films include *Faces in the Fire, Homecoming: A Vietnam Vets Journey, Searching for Home: Coming Back from War,* and *unMASKing HOPE.*

**GABRIELLE "ELLE" MARK** is an epidemiologist and a graduate of the University of Minnesota and the University of Wisconsin, La Crosse. Elle has spent a significant amount of time researching and performing health education programming surrounding the topics of mental health and wellness, as well as the prevention of mental health crises. Elle's passion for promoting mental wellness stems from her personal experience. Elle utilized her role as a local titleholder within the Miss America Organization (MAO) to share her mental health journey and help to guide others through theirs. "Growing up, I needed someone like me to tell me that it is okay to not be okay. It has become my life's mission to provide those things to others, in efforts to prevent others from experiencing the loneliness and fear a mental health disorder diagnosis can cause." You can hear Elle on her podcast, *Rank You Very Much.*

**SHOWTIME SHAWN PORTER** is a retired two-time World Champion Boxer. He was a 2007 Pan-American Team Member, as well as a 2008 Olympic Team Member. Now retired from boxing, Shawn has a flourishing career as a boxing analyst and ringside commentator working on multiple networks and platforms. He created Amateur Boxing Champions, a platform to highlight the future stars of boxing, so fans can follow and engage future world champions at the start of their career. Shawn is heavily involved with his local community of Las Vegas, Nevada. "God gave me a heart to help and after boxing, that's what I intend to do...HELP." You can hear Shawn on his podcast *The PorterWay Podcast*.

**NICOLE "NICKIE" SILVERSTEIN** is a wife and mother above all else. But before she took on those important roles, her experiences shaped her priorities for life. She was born and raised in Montana, and while Nickie loved growing up in one of the most wonderful and beautiful places, she also wanted to gain new experiences. So, she headed to Xavier University where she would receive her commission through ROTC. Nickie served nine years as an Army Finance Officer, where she served two tours in support of Operation Iraqi Freedom. Now settled down in Kansas, she continues to serve through her work with Give an Hour.

**ALLEN LEVI SIMMONS** is a United States Marine Corps Combat Veteran who has deployed to Baghdad, Iraq, and Marjah, Afghanistan. After war, Allen wrestled with PTSD from a traumatic brain injury he sustained in Afghanistan from a rocket-propelled grenade blast. He battled depression and suicide as he forged his path of purpose and inspired hope in those around him. Allen has a passion to help veterans overcome the obstacles when faced with PTSD and suicide. Allen is a published author, motivational speaker, podcaster, and entrepreneur. His first collection of poems titled *Can I Speak?* evokes empathy and inspires readers to reflect on their own unique story. His podcast *The*

*Purpose Pod* inspires and educates his listeners into their purposeful life. Allen's motto "Never Stop, Never Quit, Repeat!" has moved the hearts of those who desire motivation as they journey through life; it is a lifestyle and a mindset.

**BOB STEAD** was an Army combat medic before becoming a licensed professional counselor. The combination of Bob's life experience and academic endeavors has given him the ability to interact with people from all walks of life. Bob's unique perspective in today's divided world allows him to see people equally, and he works hard to maintain openness and honesty in all of his relationships. His passion is working with children that come from difficult places, especially those struggling with trauma. Bob enjoys helping individuals overcome the myriad of conflicts they deal with in today's ever-evolving society. Bob has a series of published children's books, including *Scrunch Your Butt Cheeks!: How little Bobby got his smile back.*

# ACKNOWLEDGMENTS

**THANK YOU, THANK YOU,**

**THANK YOU, THANK YOU....**

I first and foremost want to thank everyone at Give an Hour, Trina Clayeux, Jessica Grove, and a very special thank you to Kristin Richardson and Nickie Silverstein for bringing the "playbook" concept into the world back in 2020, when we were all isolated in our homes during Covid. Nickie, what started as a webinar series has now become a book and none of it would have been possible without you. It's been such a gift working with you, you brought joy to every single aspect of our collaboration (and you even ended up writing the story on JOY.... Look at that!)

To the Give an Hour Ambassadors, singer song-writer Bryan Abrams, documentarian Eric Christiansen, Epidemiologist Elle Mark, Champion Boxer and podcast host Showtime Shawn Porter, Combat Veteran and podcast host Allen Levi Simmons, and Combat Medic and Professional Counselor Bob Stead. Your journeys are inspiring, your courage is admirable, and the help you bring to the world is invaluable. Words cannot express how grateful I am to have your stories in this book.

Un immense merci to Dr. Anthony Puente, for your significant contribution, taking the time to read the entire manuscript and offering your compelling endorsement. It is truly an honor. Thank you to Mental Health Professional Jen Lawrence, for your invaluable assistance in reviewing the exercises and helping to craft "The Science Behind It" section.

To John O'Leary, I am beyond thrilled and still pinch myself that you wrote the foreword to this book. I can't imagine a better way for readers to start this book than by reading your inspiring story. And thank you for your "Living Inspired" podcast, you help keep us level headed, reminding us to show up with love and compassion and be more playful like our kids. A much needed message.

Jay Wang, from Southwestern Consulting, what a treat it was to reconnect after so many years! You encouraged me, gave me confidence we were headed in the right direction, and provided invaluable feedback on how to connect the dots and make it easier for the reader to follow. You are an awesome coach!!! Thank you for your generosity, your time and your guidance.

A very special thank you to husband and wife duo, Dr. Barbara Van Dahlen and Dr. Randy Phelps. I treasure all we've shared, from *A Million Little Things*, to projects with Give an Hour, and your supportive feedback on the "playbook." Heather Kam and Kimberly Williams at Vibrant Emotional Health and Ken Duckworth at NAMI, I so appreciate you making the time for me to share this idea with you when it was just that, an idea. Your psychological viewpoint was most insightful and encouraged me to forge ahead.

I am profoundly grateful for the invaluable encouragement and support from Dr. Jennifer Ashton, Dr. Dale V. Atkins, Melissa Bernstein, Miles

Borrero, Nicole Davis, Ethan Kross, Dan Jansen, Gary Mendell, Christina Moses, and Seth Serxner. Thank you for making space to graciously read these pages!

To psychotherapist, Jay D. Marson—you changed my life! Thank you for your guidance throughout the years and for introducing me to do the Impossible Future exercise back in 2003! To performance psychologist Michael Gervais, your "Finding Your Best" course is phenomenal and working with Olympic medalist turned performance coach, Nicole Davis was the cherry on top! The insights from your course are reviewed daily in my Playbook.

A huge thank you to the bold and spunky AJ Vaden from Brand Builder's Group's; you helped turn my ideas into action, introduced me to stellar tech guru and Self!sh partner, Kowsheek Mahmood, and wisely reminded me that "we all know we shouldn't judge a book by its cover but we DO!" In other words, get a designer. EJ Zebro, how grateful I am that you introduced me to graphic designer extraordinaire Riva Fischel, your timing couldn't have been better! Riva, your eye-catching designs bring beauty and clarity to a whole lotta words on the page. I adored creating with you and hope we get to do it again! To Richard Dantas, for your curiosity and suggesting we create the Self!sh Glossary!

I am so grateful for my friend Lindsay Czarniak who introduced me to Pam Long and John Nunziato of LITTLE BIG BRANDS. Pam and John, it is so exciting to be creating with you. Thank you to you both, Mark Speece, Pika Stearns, and your whole team for bringing your magic touch to the naming, cover design and branding of Self!sh.

Greatest thanks to this collaborative and generous group of ladies: Alisyn Camerota, Lauren Cohen, Kim Crawford, Jane Green, Kristin Milburn, Stefanie Lemcke, Annika Pergament, Sophie Montagnon, and Nancy Wilson for your enthusiasm and support. To my friend Jerri

Graham, I love all of our photoshoots throughout the years, and it was so special having you take the headshot for this book. Rhodie Lorenz, you are the entrepreneur who suggested we write this book! Thank you for cheering me on every step of the way and for connecting me to the writer Alli Frank. Alli, *merci beaucoup* for introducing me, a complete stranger, to your fabulous agent Liza Fleissig who is now my agent extraordinaire. To writer Emily Liebert, thank you for your friendship and suggesting Post Hill Press, the perfect fit for this book. To Debra Englander, who said YES to publishing it, to managing editor Ashlyn Inman, and to production manager Alana Mills, thank you for your enthusiasm, dedication, and guidance. Thank you to each and every one of you. A whole lotta of women supporting women!!! How fabulous!

To my acting manager and agents, Estelle Lasher, Darren Boghosian, and Scott Schachter, thank you for believing in me when no one else did. You gave me the chance to do what I love and I will forever be grateful to you. Doing this Playbook, has been a game-changer for my mental game before I get on set.... So I guess, it all ties in together nicely.

Special thanks to DJ Nash for creating *A Million Little Things*. You created this show in honor of your friend and it has touched the lives of many. Being a part of it has been the gift that keeps on giving. I am forever grateful. To my *A Million Little Things* friends, Cameron Esposito, David Giuntoli, Lizzy Greene, Chance Hurstfield, Floriana Lima, Christina Moses, Allison Miller, Grace Park, and James Roday Rodriguez. Your friendship and your support mean the world to me. It's been a privilege to work with you, learn from you, meditate with you (Christina and Allison, and yes, James, we got you to do it too—once). Christina, Allison, Floriana, and Lizzy, thank you for all our talks about mental health, for sharing the tools that work for you and for your vulnerability. Your support, your friendship, and the nature of our connection is one I will cherish forever. You exemplify what it means to show up, push through, and lift one another up.

To my dear friends, Michelle DeShon and Sarah Chapman, your support was astonishing! I can't believe you did every single exercise! Thank you for listening, for always offering your valuable insight, and for your love! Misbah Desautels, Negar Marazzi, Emmanuelle Prigent, April Book, Erica Davis, Stacey Henske, and Abbe Large, thank you for your support throughout the years, and for our lifelong friendships.

Thank you to my incredible family. I am so grateful for your guidance, and for all the love. You inspire me. A special shout out to my in-laws, Virgie and John, you are like my second parents and John, what a thrill it was to have you contribute to the conclusion of the book. To Lee, my dad, whose stories and influence are all over this book, I hope you won't mind! To Claude, my maman, you worked your whole life and showed me that I too, could be a loving, caring, present mother and still have a career. Thank you to my sons, thank you for always being you, and for not being afraid to "chat about life." For real. That brings me the greatest joy.

And, finally to my husband, Britt; "it's so much easier with two" is our motto for all house stuff but it can apply to this book too! You came up with the idea for us to create a Playbook for ourselves and look at what's happened to your idea. What a fun ride it's been. You helped me find my voice, corrected my English, and spent countless hours creating with me. I love learning with you, growing old(er), and perhaps a bit wiser too. Thank you, my love. Your dad told you circa 1992 "You and Steph, could have fun together," and I guess he was right!

# ABOUT THE AUTHOR

**Photo by Jerri Graham Photography**

**STEPHANIE SZOSTAK**, is an actress, a Give an Hour Ambassador, and speaks on overcoming failure, being an outsider, and living with authenticity.

Szostak left her native France to study business and play varsity golf at the College of William & Mary. At twenty-nine years old, after a brief stint at Chanel in New York City, she took a leap and gave the acting world a try. Her most notable projects include *The Devil Wears*

*Prada, Iron Man 3, Dinner for Schmucks*, and the ABC hit series *A Million Little Things*.

Ten years into her career, she suffered from crippling imposter syndrome which pushed her to address her mindset and develop her own Playbook as a daily practice of mental fitness. She hopes your *Self!sh* Playbook will support your journey of discovery, learning and growth.